# THE CROSSING

An Epic Testimony of Jesus Christ

HOLIDAY

Copyright © 2024 by Holiday

All rights reserved.

No part of this book may be reproduced in any form or by any means, electronic, mechanical, photocopying, recording or otherwise, without permission of the publisher.

ISBN: 979-8-218-37835-6

Bismarck, North Dakota, United States

## Dedicated to

*the Lord Jesus Christ,
the Captain of our salvation.
(Heb. 2:10)*

# Contents

INTRODUCTION . . . . . . . . . . . . . . . . . . . . . . . . . . . . . . . . . . . 5

PROLOGUE . . . . . . . . . . . . . . . . . . . . . . . . . . . . . . . . . . . . . . . 9

I.     EXILES OF BABEL . . . . . . . . . . . . . . . . . . . . . . . . . . . 10

II.    THE SACRIFICE . . . . . . . . . . . . . . . . . . . . . . . . . . . . 23

III.   THE PROPHET'S REPORT . . . . . . . . . . . . . . . . . . . . . 32

IV.   THE VALLEY OF NIMROD . . . . . . . . . . . . . . . . . . . . 41

V.    THE PILLAR . . . . . . . . . . . . . . . . . . . . . . . . . . . . . . . 52

VI.   JOURNEY FROM THE VALLEY OF NIMROD . . . . . . . . . . 61

VII.  MOUNT ZERIN . . . . . . . . . . . . . . . . . . . . . . . . . . . . . 71

VIII. THE SHORES OF THE OCEAN . . . . . . . . . . . . . . . . . . 82

IX.   BUILDING THE ARKS . . . . . . . . . . . . . . . . . . . . . . . . 93

X.    ORAH . . . . . . . . . . . . . . . . . . . . . . . . . . . . . . . . . . . . 107

XI.   SHELEM . . . . . . . . . . . . . . . . . . . . . . . . . . . . . . . . . . 118

XII.  PRAYER FOR LIGHT . . . . . . . . . . . . . . . . . . . . . . . . . 128

XIII. LADING . . . . . . . . . . . . . . . . . . . . . . . . . . . . . . . . . . 137

XIV. LAST EVE ASHORE . . . . . . . . . . . . . . . . . . . . . . . . . . 145

XV.  THE VOYAGE . . . . . . . . . . . . . . . . . . . . . . . . . . . . . . 156

XVI. ARRIVAL . . . . . . . . . . . . . . . . . . . . . . . . . . . . . . . . . 170

APPENDIX . . . . . . . . . . . . . . . . . . . . . . . . . . . . . . . . . . . . . 177

# INTRODUCTION

We are facing difficult days. Numerous threats are at work in every nation on earth. If we were inclined, we might compile a long list of the challenges and dangers which characterize our time and impose upon our general happiness and security. Perhaps, apart from short periods of reprieve, it has always been this way everywhere. The fallen nature of mankind combined with the dark endeavors of men like Cain and Nimrod are the systemic mechanisms of degeneracy, dissolution, and destruction in our world. Their myopic lust for power and the oppressions they foment make the world a very unpleasant place for many.

This poem was written especially for the meek and humble followers of righteousness. It is for those who are fighting battles of discouragement and fear. It is for the desperate and despairing, who know not where to turn for help. It is for those beneath the millstone of poverty. You are dearly loved by your Heavenly Father. He knows you intimately and is perfectly aware of your personal struggles, your sufferings, and disappointments. I composed this poem to encourage you in faith and hope. Your afflictions will refine you and make you fit for the Kingdom of God, if you endure them well, trusting in the Lord, Jesus Christ. If God has brought you to an experience of suffering, He will bring you through that suffering, for He has all power to save and to redeem you to His presence. Your ultimate goal is the eternal life for which you enlisted as a child of God in a premortal setting. You can reach that destination, but you can do so only under the arm of Jesus Christ. Trust in Him. This is the primary theme of *The Crossing, An Epic Testimony of Jesus Christ.*

I believe that the Gospel of Jesus Christ was taught to Adam and Eve and to their posterity. Salvation has always been exclusively centered in Christ. He is the Lamb chosen before the foundation of the world. The law of sacrifice was revealed by God as a prophetic ordinance instituted to direct the minds and hearts of the earliest generations to the One whom our Heavenly Father would send to redeem mankind from the effects of the Fall. From the beginning, many found it difficult to exercise the faith required by the Gospel and to keep the commandments of God. Many were led astray by Satan, who inspired the establishment of counterfeit religions, which were attractive because of their permissiveness. There has always been one divinely-authorized path to our highest potential, which is eternal life, and that path is Christ and the laws and ordinances He has revealed.

I have written much poetry, but I consider *The Crossing* to be my magnum opus and the poem I have wanted to publish before any other. Its creation through a period of challenging years has afforded me many intense moments of profound joy and gratitude. It represents an earnest struggle to find language worthy of my deepest feelings, the life, and light of my soul. That height and power of language were too often beyond my reach, as the reader will discover. But occasionally, words and expressions above my natural ability were given to me by the power of the Holy Ghost, and I am thankful to my Heavenly Father for His kindness in so blessing me. Readers will recognize the contrast. I have only wanted to bear my certain testimony that Jesus Christ is our Savior and Redeemer, the Only Begotten Son of our Heavenly Father. This witness runs with my blood and electrifies my nerves. It is the rock upon which I stand and the cloak around my shoulders.

My art seems to grow out of a coincidence of influences, observations, and experiences. The imperative to write originates for me at the conjunction of new perception and inspired consciousness. In 1988, I was engaged in a personal study of every ancient account I could find on the subject of the confusion of tongues at the time of the destruction of the Tower of Babel. I was then intrigued by the brief record of this era found in the Holy Bible and by a related story abridged in the Book of Mormon. In my searching, I was surprised and delighted to discover that the fundamental outlines of this history are well-attested in several ancient texts, and I have quoted from a few of these sources in an Appendix at the end of this work. During the same period, I happened to read an excellent issue of National Geographic, which was wholly devoted to the beauty of the land of Australia. (Portraits of the Land, Feb. 1988). Frankly, I was heart-struck by four lines of poetry from the poem "Bellbirds" by Henry C. Kendall, appended to an evocative picture of a verdant mountain scene:

> By channels of coolness the echoes are calling,
> And down the dim gorges I hear the creek falling;
> It lives in the mountain, where moss and the sedges
> Touch with their beauty the banks and the ledges;
> **(First published in** *"Leaves from Australian Forest,"* **1869)**

Under the power of Kendall's verse, I wondered if its amphibrachic form might be an appropriate medium through which I could elaborate the feelings impressed upon me by the prophet Ether's abridged history of one of the emigrant groups which survived the calamity at Babel. This account is contained in the Book of Mormon. I determined to make an attempt and within a very brief time wrote the opening lines of *The Crossing:*

> Between the two rivers, near wind-raveled Babel,
> Despaired a spared people, preparing to travel
> Away from the rabble and widely-strewn rubble,
> Remnants of heaven-sent wreckage and trouble.

*The Crossing* is about a community of families, who abandon Babel at the time of its destruction and migrate over a challenging span of years to a promised land, led, sustained, empowered, and protected by the Lord Jesus Christ. It is intended to be a metaphor of man's journey through mortal life, expressing how the Savior enables us to overcome every impediment that keeps us from reaching our highest potential. My faith and experience have taught me that there is nothing we cannot overcome by the grace of Jesus Christ. *We are redeemed through the Mighty One's merit.* That is the central message of this poem. Inasmuch as we place our trust in God and keep His commandments, He will bless us and guide us through our troubles and trials and will ultimately bring us to eternal life in His presence with our families.

> The Sailor cannot see the North
> But knows the Needle can.
> **(Emily Dickinson, Ltr. #265 to T.W. Higginson)**

As for historical accuracy, I freely admit that some of the poem falls within the category of "what may have happened." It is poetic conjecture and elaboration without any intention of offending my friends, the purists, who prefer strict residence within the boundaries of written revelation. I trust that we will one day possess the full record of those ancient days and be able to become fully acquainted with the principal protagonists and antagonists of the period briefly covered in *The Crossing*. What I have created is certainly no substitute for the books of holy scripture comprising the standard works of the Church of Jesus Christ of Latter-day Saints. I hope that my poem will cause some to search the revealed word more faithfully, more carefully, seeking to know more fully the character and commandments of the Most High and to bring their lives into complete harmony with the divine will. I have sought to write plainly and without the abstraction and obscurity that so often confuses readers of contemporary poetry. A smudged meaning cannot edify anyone. In those instances where I have failed in plainness, I deeply apologize. Please forgive my weakness in writing. I have sought earnestly for the assistance of the Holy Ghost in bearing testimony of the Savior of all mankind. The labor of composing *The Crossing* has been a spiritual journey for me, an exercise of intense prayer, through which I have realized the blessing given to them of old as recorded in the Book of Moses: *"For it was given unto as many as called upon God to write by the spirit of inspiration."* (6:5b) Line upon line, precept upon precept, here a little and there a little, the Lord blessed me. I now share that blessing with the world, inviting all to come unto Christ, our Redeemer, and in doing so, I hope my Lord will consider this poem to be an acceptable offering unto Him.

Holiday

Thanksgiving, 2023

# PROLOGUE

O whispering Spirit,
move softly again
upon the face of my deep.
Overspread my formless voids,
and warmly brood
upon the vast expanse
of my darkness.
Be still with me, thy vessel.
Where empty, permeate and plenish;
where desolate, make fertile, fruitful.
Be one with me once more
to bear the light of truth!

# I
# EXILES OF BABEL

Between the two rivers, near wind-raveled Babel,
Despaired a spared people, preparing to travel
Away from the rabble and widely-strewn rubble,
Remnants of heaven-sent wreckage and trouble.

Here, twenty-four families camped in a cluster,
Adjusting to homelessness after the bluster
That leveled their dwellings and left them no shelter.
Babel had fallen; the Holy One felled her.

So suddenly fallen! The City of Splendor;
The grandeur of Sumer; a baseborn pretender;
An idol-wed bride of detested obsessions,
Punished because of her grievous transgressions.

So suddenly fallen! All ripped and uprooted.
A city of silken pretension now muted.
How swiftly the huffing of fools is defeated;
Feasting corruption and priestcraft unseated!

So suddenly fallen! All gloss and vainglory
Consumed by a ruinous windstorm. As surely
As prophets had warned them, the awful doom followed.
Finely dressed falseness was swept up and swallowed.

What now her proverbial riches and power?
What now of her haughty, contemptuous tower?
What now of her fables and idols and cavil?
How thou art fallen from honor, O Babel!

Not far from the downfall of prideful sedition,
The downfall and rout of a ripened ambition,
A freed congregation, afraid and afflicted,
Waited, preserved from the blight of the wicked.

These few from their city's confounded were singled.
Now homeless and humbled, they sadly commingled
In sapping despondency, hopelessly fading,
Bent in the gray of adversity's shading.

Necessity tied them like exiles of conquest.
Yet lacking the knit and the knot of true oneness,
They languished at standstill and argued like strangers,
Wanting direction to guide them through dangers.

While some voices grumbled, disturbing the younger,
Complaining of losses and hardship and hunger,
Undaunted stood Jared, all stresses enduring,
Murmuring not, and the others assuring.

While eating his dinner, he pondered his choices,
Too near to avoid overhearing those voices
Of frightened and world-weary friends from the city,
Tasting the bitter and stirring his pity.

Accustomed to cumbersome burdens and labor,
With worthy hands calloused like kiln-fired clayware,
He worked with a purpose as perils grew graver,
Blessing his family as well as his neighbor.

He worked with his might for the care of the people,
Who looked to his lodestone resolve, as a needle
Magnetic will point to the northern direction.
Moving among them with friendly affection,

He ministered kindness and warmhearted humor,
Attending their needs as they tented in Sumer
Away from the ruins of human perversion,
Service his nature despite the dispersion.

Now, Jared, to honor an earlier epoch,
Was given the name of the father of Enoch.
His mother had said of the godsend she tended:
"Straight from a loftier place he descended."

The Lord had endowed him with power in body
And towering stature, though Jared was godly
In goodness of spirit as well as appearance,
Showing his merit by faithful adherence

To all that the prophets proclaimed in their teaching.
He listened as men of the Priesthood were preaching
In Babel, believing their words and forewarning,
Sick in his heart at the mocking and scorning

They heard in reply from the mouths of the wicked.
He knew that the discipline prophets predicted
Would come – they would forfeit the language of Adam.
God would amend them so they could not fathom

The meaning or sense of their old conversation,
Confounding their oneness of language to chasten
The city for sin. He responded discreetly,
Trusting the witness of prophets completely.

Now gratitude moved in his blood. He considered
Their safety and freedom and faith, unembittered,
Subdued at the edge of the vast desolation
Seen in the sunset. For since the cessation

Of furious winds on the city, he marveled
At all the upheaval, the language now garbled,
Discerning the wonderful windfall effected,
Mindful that he and his own were protected.

Downcast was the tower but never his temper.
His natural faith was a spiritual ember
Of courage through outrage and rages repeated,
Suffering difficult days undefeated.

He let his reflections return to another,
By name, Moriancumer, more than a brother –
So pure, if he offered a prayer in the Spirit,
Surely, his Father in heaven would hear it.

His brother, though younger, was one of the prophets
Rejected and scorned by the hard-hearted scofflets
Of Babel. In service to God, he was zealous,
Braving his duty to warn the rebellious.

To him in humility, Jared resorted
Before the Great Storm, and with purpose reported
His hope that Jehovah would never divide them,
Hope that the cursing would never betide them.

He bade Moriancumer, "Cry unto heaven,
And plead with the Lord to respect us as brethren,
And let us remember the speech we have spoken,
Keeping in mercy our closeness unbroken."

And then, Moriancumer cried to the Father
With faith in the faith and the hope of his brother
That God, if entreated, would grant their petition,
Sparing them both from distress of division.

The Lord in compassion did hear his petition
And honored that prayer and His servants' submission,
Bestowing the blessing desired by the brothers,
Giving them faith to solicit for others.

God favored a prayer that the prophet propounded
That friends with their children would not be confounded
But also, would share in their ancient advantage,
Keeping their voice in the beautiful language

In which all their records and scriptures were written.
Their Books of Remembrance with mysteries hidden,
Containing the sayings of seers and sages,
Bearing the truth of the earliest ages,

Were sealed from the souls of the rebels confounded.
The words of the prophets they doubted now sounded
Bizarre to their ears, to their minds unfamiliar.
Those not believing that God would bewilder

Their oneness of tongue, as He spoke in forewarning,
Who joked at His servants with scurrilous scorning,
Awoke to the cost of their foolish derision,
Wrung when the Holy One sent His division.

Thus Jared, his brother, and those they befriended
Took kindness in common, as heaven extended
Those blessings of language the prophet requested,
Bonds of alliance from others divested.

The man Moriancumer, brother of Jared,
In features akin, in demeanor disparate,
Sat holding a youngster, contented and yawning,
Under a sycamore's leafy-green awning.

With eyelids unopened, he cradled the weanling
And lullabied softly, while quietly gleaning
A measure of solace himself from the caring,
Easing the burden of stress he was bearing.

Composed in his comfort, the little one slumbered,
Her forehead unmarked by the fear that encumbered
The hearts of the fathers and mothers there gathered.
O to be calm when calamity battered!

Then laying her blissfully limp on a wrapper,
A sheepskin unsheared he unrolled for the napper,
He saw that his precious was peacefully nested,
Kissing the blush of her cheeks as she rested.

Her mellowing innocence softened the hour
And granted the overspent outcast the power
To smile for the present though stark seemed the morrow,
Stark and uncertain and darkened with sorrow.

When resolute Jared had finished his eating,
He came with a smile and embrace for a greeting,
And, after the hesitant circle surveying,
Spoke to his brother with heartiness, saying:

"My brother, I love you with endless devotion.
As bronze are we bonded, forever unbroken.
Like copper and tin, fast alloyed in the furnace,
Fused by a fire that could bind but not burn us.

Our families have suffered profound persecution
From devils beguiled by the Builder's delusion.
For we were in bondage and bullied by lashing,
Pressed like the bricks they compelled us to fashion.

But now, my dear brother, my joy is unbounded!
Though banished with friends from the city he founded,
By prayer we are blessed above Babel's late builders.
Wilderness-sown, them the Lord now bewilders.

For we have retained the pure tongue of our parents.
Our whole-hearted worship this gift of words warrants,
Bestowed from above, but abused by the worldly,
Taken from scoffers, profane and unworthy.

Now challenge our friends the delay of our transfer,
Annoying me daily, demanding an answer.
But what can I say when they ask in frustration:
Whither the way to our new habitation?

Look round us and see how our people are stricken,
How sorely we need inspiration to quicken
Our pulses and rally our pale aspirations,
Hope to redeem us from exile's vexations.

But you, Moriancumer, you can illumine
Our path through the Spirit, for you have communion
With God, whom you worship with all of your being.
Surely, the Lord will respond to your pleading.

He will as He has on those other occasions,
Who heard and preserved our revered conversations.
Now one who would notice and know must discover,
You are the Tower of Babel, my brother!

Go, offer a lamb to our Father in Heaven,
And cry to the Lord for a land to be given
Where we, unconfounded, can live our religion,
Far from Confusion's infernal dominion,

Away from the pester-apostate and despot,
A better estate than this borderland respite.
Select from the best of our flock in the pasture.
Sacrifice; seek from our Heavenly Father."

The brother of Jared, a man large and mighty,
A prophet of God, for his faith favored highly,
Whose pleas for his people drew Godly forbearance,
Saving their language at Babel's disturbance,

Just listened with glistening eyes to his brother,
Attentive and smiling, not able to smother
The heart-filling flames of fraternal affection
Adding a glow to his placid complexion.

He wept from the wealth of his spirit's deep wellspring
Pure treasures of tears with emotions upswelling,
Unspoken soaked syllables, eye-spilled wet letters,
Fluent, true feelings expressed without fetters.

The Spirit's influence induced this outflowing,
A soul-centered fountain of eloquence growing.
Imbued was his beard by this liberal tearfall,
Rivers of rapture on features so cheerful!

While feeling the sensible press of the Spirit
And calling on wisdom extended and wearied,
The prophet, his accents of kindness conveying,
Echoed his brother's encouragement, saying:

"Dear Jared, please hear me, my friend and my brother.
Your love, oft-expressed as from father and mother,
Has lifted my difficult life like a windlass,
Raising my hope when our happenstance pinned us.

Impressed is my soul by your service essential,
The boon of true brotherhood's goodly potential.
In wisdom and kindliness, you are distinguished.
Know my affection remains undiminished.

The confidence you have reposed in me, Jared,
Has strengthened the strings of my courage through varied
Experience during our days in oppression.
O to be able to make an expression

Of all that I feel for you, pillar of friendship!
What fortune that I have been near you in kinship
And blessed by your faith in our living Redeemer.
Being your brother has made my life sweeter.

My brother, permit me to share my conviction
That good will ensue from this kiss of affliction.
I know not the purpose of God for our people,
What He might do with us freed from the evil

We suffered through Nimrod's perverse insurrection.
But He is the Father of truth and perfection
And will in His wisdom unbosom his purpose
When He is ready. We need not be nervous.

For we will be nurtured from hour to hour
By faith in our Savior, our fountain of power.
He knows our predicament here by the river,
Knows we are needful, knows how to deliver

And will, if we trust Him; of this I am certain.
Then work to encourage each murmuring person.
We'll wait on the Lord God of Enoch and Noah,
Settling our hope in the love of Jehovah.

As kin to the Heavenly King and entitled
To light through the privilege with which we have trifled,
This people as one should entreat the Eternal,
Asking our Father to steer our dispersal.

We all should appeal to the King of Creation
To bring us as one from these straits of frustration,
For He is a God of compassion and pity,
Though in His wrath He made waste of the city.

Encourage our people to send their desires
On high, as the God of our fathers requires.
Invite them to pray in the name of our Savior,
Meekly in faith to our Lord and Creator,

Returning their thanks for the blessings provided.
Our circle is not by His anger divided,
Though other divisions among us are growing.
Let us give thanks for what God is bestowing.

Yea, urge our companions to pray with their children,
And after this duty we owe is fulfilled, then
Assuredly God in His mercy will answer.
Truly the Almighty God is the granter

Of peace and of wisdom to all who will hearken
To Him, who will humble themselves and not darken
Their hearts by obeying their carnal desires.
Scriptures repeat that the Spirit inspires

The humble, who offer their faith-filled petitions
To Father. He loves us! He sees, and He listens.
He cares for our small congregation of Christians.
Each of our people should plead for assistance.

Now Jared, my brother, admonish our people
To call on the Lord in this galling upheaval.
For I do believe, if our prayers are united,
God will regard, and our way will be lighted.

Tomorrow while fasting, I'll walk to seclusion
To worship and sacrifice my contribution
Of faith to our Father, beseeching His guidance,
Seeking His will for our homeless alliance."

"My thanks for your wisdom, my brother," said Jared.
"My thanks for your confident words and warm-hearted
Encouragement, spoken with accents impressive,
Witnessed as true by the Spirit attestive.

Now, I will return to our murmuring circle
And quiet their qualms in this fearful reversal
By sharing the favors of faith you extended,
Urging their prayers to the One you commended.

And know on the morrow, I also am fasting
In suppliant prayer to our God everlasting
To ask for the grace of the place He would plant us,
Plead for direction to land He would grant us."

Then smiling, he turned from his brother and parted
With radiant hope from the one he regarded
As noble as Noah, the Comfort of promise.
Knowing the balm of empowering calm is

A gift of the Spirit of God and a blessing
Essential in crosswinds of temporal testing,
The brother of good Moriancumer carried
Courage by word to his people, who tarried

In tar pits of spiritless fear and confusion.
And there through the evening, he strove to unloosen
Delusions of impotence glooming awareness,
Sparking their spirits to bloom in the spareness.

# II
# THE SACRIFICE

What glories attended the sun's resurrection!
What colors in clouds! Lo, the glow of perfection
In newborn uniqueness! Once there and then shifted,
Gracing through moments of morning as gifted.

The waters reflected those glistering graces,
The splendors of heaven that sunshine unlaces,
As meek Moriancumer washed in the river,
Grooming to worship the glorious Giver.

Observing the counsel of Jared, his brother,
The prophet departed to offer another
Consuming expression of priestly devotion,
Humbly the gift of the First to foretoken.

He took the essentials his task would require –
A knife for the sacrifice, coals for the fire,
A bundle of tinder and sticks for the altar,
Lastly, an offering, free from its halter.

He left the encampment to plead for compassion
And offer a sacrifice after the fashion
Revealed unto Adam and Eve beyond Eden,
Whence they were driven when death fruit was eaten.

When Adam and Eve were shut out from God's presence,
And freed in their bodies for liberty's lessons,
The Lord from the Garden commanded the curstlings:
"Worship the Father, and offer your firstlings."

And they were observant, not knowing the reasons,
When after the trials of several seasons,
An angel appeared and inquired of the kneelers,
"Why do you sacrifice Godward these creatures?"

Addressing the messenger, Adam was candid:
"I know not the purpose, save God hath commanded.
That God hath commanded for me is sufficient.
Faith will I place in my Father omniscient."

The angel gave answer: "This thing is a semblance
Our Father appointed to bring to remembrance
The Only Begotten, foredestined to suffer.
Types of His life-giving sacrifice offer."

An innocent emblem, unblemished in figure,
Attended the brother of Jared with vigor,
Who walked with an easy and reverent amble,
Legging along with his perfect example.

Untethered, the substitute followed its shepherd,
A life for the brother of Jared to jeopard,
A precious, affectionate friend freely rendered,
So like the Son by the Father engendered.

Not long they attained their serene destination,
A pine-spiring hill of sublime isolation,
With mossy-soft carpeted slopes gently ramping,
Wildflowers' rich multiplicity sampling.

Ascending the hillside embroidered with flowers,
On up through the shadows of sheltering bowers,
The worshipper climbed with his lamb to a clearing,
Sunlight's empyreal splendor appearing.

Bright autumn's meridian temper brought calmness,
Reminding the prophet of Enoch's sure promise
That One in the noontime of mortal duration,
Dying would quicken the day of salvation.

Of pure stock cross-bred for superior power,
The lamb on the hillside was suffered to scour
The earth, full-deferring with single submission,
Meek to the shepherd's all-wise supervision.

While scanning the landscape, he saw widely scattered
His hard-weathered harvest of stones to be gathered,
Ensoiled like the children of men in probation,
Types of the multitudes needing salvation.

By able exertion, the Elder selected
From broken and crestfallen rocks and erected
Of this congregation an altar well-fitted,
Stonework as weighty as sin unremitted.

His love for his Shepherd brought thoughts of another,
The keeper of sheep, who was slain by his brother,
When Cain in conspiracy kindled in anger,
Greatly inspired by that Satan, whose rancor

Ran back to the Council where Father rejected
His arrogant offer to save, yet respected
The selfless and excellent gift of another,
Praised the submission of Lucifer's brother.

For Abel made altars as Adam had taught him
And took from the best of his firstlings and brought them
For sacrifice, each a memorial tendered,
Teaching the gospel of Him who surrendered

To save us. By shedding His blood, He did save us.
By bearing our sins and transgressions He gave us
The way to the presence of God through repentance,
Ripping the veil that prevented our entrance.

With wormwood to kindle a crosswork of cypress,
Arranged in its order to cremate the likeness,
That simplified mount for the sacrifice founded
Roused him with sorrow and gladness compounded.

A sorrow for innocence brought to the altar
And tears for the Servant, whose love would not falter
To bear the unmerited pangs of an anguish
Due to the guilty, who'd otherwise languish.

Lo, He is our joy and the sacrifice given
For gladness! To life by His blood, we are bidden;
To life by His death, we are surely delivered.
Joy is the gospel the offering prefigured.

He called to the lamb, and the lamb heard him calling
And came to the altar, not halting or stalling,
But quick to the beckoning voice of the Master,
Straight to the gesturing palm of the Pastor.

The prime of his well-beloved flock fixed for slaughter!
A truthful similitude stilled on the altar,
A shadow ordained by a glorious priesthood,
Shedding its mortal red blood on the tree wood.

He followed the law as Jehovah commanded
And suffered those vinegar minutes red-handed,
Alight with indelible thoughts of the Righteous,
Offered in brotherly love to unite us

As children of joy with our heavenly parents.
He knew from the records the many declarants,
Who testified clearly of Christ our Redeemer,
Named as the mercy for every believer.

He flayed his replacement soon after the slaying,
Adjacent the altar the sheepskin arraying,
A fleecy, white pelt for apparel intended,
Gaining an aid from the life he had ended,

Reminding the prophet of raiment provided
By God in the garden, where Adam resided,
Replacing those aprons of fig leaves with garments
Tailored from skins for our primeval parents.

That redress prepared by the Savior attested
Endowments of power and right in Him vested
To cover our spirits and cover our errors,
Sparing God's offspring from death and its terrors.

The sunlight was darkened by clouds that had drifted.
The body lay dreadful on altar uplifted,
Blood-red, as if robed in a cover of scarlet,
Stripped and outstretched on the wood set to char it.

He sprinkled some salt on the offering as precious.
(The Sacrifice serves to preserve and to bless us),
Suggesting the sweating of blood by our Savior,
Pain He would suffer to bring us in favor

With Father again to our gain in His glory.
How precious! Without that atonement, the jury
Of justice and death would condemn us forever,
Ever the spirit from body dissever.

As feelings of woe and of wrenching distended,
And smoke from the smoldering victim ascended,
He knelt down to pray on the cushion of sheepskin,
Lifting his hands to the heavens while weeping.

He poured out his soul-cry of tearful thanksgiving
And offered himself as a sacrifice living.
His prayer was a struggle of mighty expansions,
Seeking compassion for kin and companions.

And long he continued his cries unto heaven,
While clarity rare by the Spirit was given,
When suddenly issued the blessing of blessings,
Hearing the voice of his Savior addressing!

And thus, spoke the Savior to Jared's dear brother:
"Your cries for compassion are heard by our Father.
Go; gather your creatures, each kind and creation,
Seed of all sorts and supplies for migration.

Assemble with Jared your wives and your children.
Your friends with their families, bid them all welcome.
And when you are ready to head the endeavor,
Lead them forth northward, agreeing together.

Remove to the Valley of Nimrod and tarry.
From my narrow pathway, take care not to vary.
And there I will meet you to take you to Eden.
Going before you, your Shepherd and Beacon.

Yea, travel from Babel! No longer inhabit
This land of rebellion. Forsake her that added
Black slime to her bricks of iniquity daily.
Travel from Babel, but seek to avail ye

Of every essential and every provision
Your wisdom commands for a long expedition.
Let all be prepared ere you start your departure.
Take from the city necessities harder

To make or to find in a wilderness setting,
Your tents and utensils and tools not forgetting.
The end of your mission is many days distant.
Gather then all you may need and sufficient.

Because of your mighty and long supplication,
Of you and your seed I will raise a great nation,
Where Adam, the Ancient of Days, tilled his garden,
Gladdened with Eve for my promise of pardon.

Where Havilah, wholly encompassed by Pison,
Was gorgeous with onyx and gold, and pure Gihon,
Euphrates, and Hiddekel parted direction,
Flowing like music from Eden's perfection.

Where Enoch, the Lad, led my saints like a lion,
Who flourished in glory with pure hearts in Zion,
When mountains did flee, and the wicked did cower,
Trembling before the Seer's terrible power.

Where Noah, the seed-saving preacher, gave warning
To ripe generations, ungodly and scorning.
That Comfort, whose ark was uplifted by flooding,
Raised to deliver, my offering foreboding.

A land once corrupted, defiled by perversion,
Accursed to the wicked, then cleansed by immersion,
Reserved for the righteous who worship in Spirit,
Zion's foundation, which you will inherit.

Return to my people, and take these good tidings.
Invite their repentance from sins and backslidings.
Let each make his promise to cease from dissension,
Shun straining tensions and taint of contention.

Obedient saints are the seeds of my sowing,
The plants of my planting, and where they are growing
I'll joy in the fruit that will follow their fielding,
Smile on the excellent yield of their yielding."

The prophet returned to his camping companions,
So feathered by cheer he might drift over canyons,
Unmindful of time or the sights of existence,
Heedless of need, as he hastened the distance.

# III
# THE PROPHET'S REPORT

The humbled uprooted with Jared soon gathered
Beneath a full moon to a meeting that mattered -
To hear Moriancumer's thrilling recital.
Word from the Lord through a prophet is vital!

It looked like the prophet partook of some potion
Inducing a breathless and headlong emotion
Uncommon among these so solemn and somber,
Strange for a man who was normally calmer!

There stood Moriancumer, red and disheveled,
And traces of blood from the sacrifice speckled
The tarnish of ashes and dust on his clothing.
Passion his presence! as though he were floating

On thought-clouds excited by lightning and thunder.
Provoked by his visage and soaked in the wonder
Of anticipation, the audience trembled.
These were his words to the people assembled:

"Dear brothers and sisters, draw hither and listen,
And I shall recite how my hope has arisen
To lighten my dim and delimited vision,
Mending my fear-blinded mind with bold wisdom.

With faith in the Lord, meekly thanking and thirsting,
I knelt with my shins on the skin of the firstling
And poured out my heart at the threshold of heaven,
Fervently questing the Spirit's pure leaven.

Again, God has spoken with whispering power
And answered my prayer in the worshipping hour
With peaceable words and such wonderful solace,
Hearing my cries and fulfilling His promise.

He hears all the prayers of His sons and His daughters,
Commanding our worship not only at altars,
But always, with all of our hearts never feigning.
Call upon Father in faith till attaining.

Beseeching the Lord, I received an assurance
Of heaven's intent to reward our endurance
Of trials by faith with the gift of a nation,
Promising land which is far from this station –

The sanctified land where the archangel Michael,
As Adam embodied, began a new cycle,
For joy and for children becoming a mortal,
Freely transgressing to open life's portal.

The land where the Serpent deceived our First Mother,
Evoking bereavement till word of One Other
Evinced the great plan for all mankind's retrieval,
Ever relieving our parents primeval.

The land where the City of Zion was founded,
When Enoch, the seventh from Adam, astounded
The blood-drunken world with an unconquered concord,
Oneness in all, which the Lord strongly honored.

Three hundred and sixty-five years it abided,
A city of peace, where Jehovah resided,
Till Enoch and all of his people were taken,
Planted in heaven, this planet forsaking;

Reserved to return at the latter-day burning,
When all of the godly are gathered and yearning
To fellowship brothers and sisters of Zion,
Even the saints from the orbs of Orion.

Think not that the Lord has forsaken our circle
And spurns all imperiled by Babel's dispersal.
The chosen are chastened to stir their contrition,
Soul-spurred to satisfy mercy's condition.

Believe in our living and loving Redeemer,
Who frees from captivity. Let us give deeper
Devotion and ripen in righteousness daily,
Thus overcome all enslavement and frailty.

Believe in the First of our Father Eternal,
For He is our Helper and Savior Supernal.
Believe that He loves us with love everlasting.
Prove this, my witness, with prayerful fasting.

Refreshen your senses; confess your transgressions,
And call upon Father with humble expressions.
Receive a remission of sins through repentance.
Pray to be pure for the Spirit's attendance.

The Holy Messiah shall make intercession
And open the gate to eternal progression.
Then let us rely on His mercy and merit,
Thereby the Kingdom of Heaven inherit.

Rejoice then, you Daystars! You children of glory!
Be cheerful and fearless! O, why should we worry?
For have we not read in the Book of Remembrance:
Blessings shall come if we keep the commandments?

Encouragement take from the records engraven
On plates, as ordained by Our Father in Heaven,
The sacred account since the seasons Edenic,
Writ or collected for scripture by Enoch.

Take heart like the chosen with Enos, who started
From bloodshed in Shulon to blessings imparted
By God in a country of promise named Cainan,
Thereby escaping the raging of Satan.

Remember Methuselah! Remnant of Zion,
Who left that bright city to bring forth the scion
Foreshown unto Enoch by glorious vision.
Ponder how bold that sage Elder's decision!

Such valiancy! Quitting the city ascendant!
Imagine him leaving that kingdom resplendent,
Outshining in glory all worldly alliance,
Nigh unto heaven by Gospel compliance.

From home, where the power of godliness quickened,
To spots, where the blot of apostasy sickened,
Methuselah moved with the news of salvation,
Viewing the wonder of Zion's translation.

If dauntless that hero could face the horizon,
Exchanging for sorrow the rapture of Zion,
Then we without fear can show heels to this squalor,
Heeding the Lord with devotion and valor.

Recall from our scriptures those giants malignant,
Who threatened the life of that prophet benignant,
Whom God didst empower with priesthood eternal:
Noah, pursued by those monsters infernal.

That teacher of righteousness prayed for protection
From war-minded tribes, who received no correction.
And Noah found grace, when he placed his reliance
Firmly in God, who preserved him from giants."

Then pausing, the patriarch peered at the faces
Of bleary-eyed parents, whose brows bore the traces
Of wrinkles and creases by stresses imprinted.
Torch-lit, the tears on each countenance glinted.

The prophet then said to his rapt congregation:
"O, may we not faint in the time of temptation,
When trials and hardship sit harsh on our shoulders.
Faith can diminish the weight of those boulders

Of trouble our Teacher may call us to carry.
Should Satan attempt with his cohorts to harry
And harrow our souls, as he did unto Noah,
Faith in the name of the son of Eloah

Will strengthen and save us. Then let us be faithful
To God in our travels, no matter how scatheful
The circumstance facing our venturing circle.
Stand upon faith in our Father Eternal!

His eyes are upon us. His ears are attentive.
Attempts to approach Him at times apprehensive,
Like this one, are surely accepted with favor.
Pray, and His presence will help us be braver.

Our choices will fashion precise definitions
Of us, of our spirits, amid oppositions
Set forth for our sakes from the morn of creation —
Nature's adversity, Satan's temptation,

The favor of God and availments of nature,
Together persistently nighing as neighbor
To neighbor in wonderful contrast and color,
Testing our preference — failure or valor.

Beloved believers, the Lord bade me mention:
Beware that none wrangle nor kindle contention.
For only by love is the Spirit invited.
Covenants make to be kind and united.

Yes, love one another; let love be the keystone
That keeps us united and strong in our seasons
Together.  With love we have pinions to fly on.
Love can attain the environs of Zion.

As you would be treated, so treat you the others,
And minister one to another as brothers
And sisters by caring, unselfish expressions,
Sharing in charity all your possessions.

Remember, be virtuous, kind and forgiving.
A wealth of well-being in sunlight of living
Will cover the one, who can serve with the sermon,
Honoring God while perfecting his person.

Then waken tomorrow at earliest dayglow,
And gather together our flocks from the meadow
With creatures and plant seed in character varied.
Furnish the wagons with goods to be carried.

Then onward, my strong ones, and we will rely on
The Only Begotten, whose throne is in Zion,
Where nothing but beauty with truth is accepted!
Onward and bid all our steps be intrepid!"

The prophet thus finished reporting his message
Received from the Savior in words that did presage
A beautiful future, a fullness of glory,
Stored for the righteous who strive to be holy.

And near him his children with nephews and nieces
Were seated consoled by their warm, wholesome pieces
Of newly-baked seedcakes besweetened with honey –
Food for these refugees camped in the country.

A savory portion of breadstuff still steamy,
All covered with butter, full-flavored, and creamy,
Was brought with a gourd cup of river-chilled water
Up to the man in the hands of a daughter.

How welcome the taste of that wilderness serving!
A supper to conquer their hunger unnerving,
Each morsel restoring their courage and humor,
Turning their minds from the tables of Sumer.

He reached out to each of his well-cherished children,
Perceiving their need by the Spirit that filled him,
And blessed them with kisses and caring caresses,
Loving relief from life's fear-filling stresses.

The soft-hearted father encouraged his darlings
And bade their avoidance of tussles and snarlings,
Persuading his young ones to serve one another.
Each was admonished to honor his mother.

Embracing the children around him encircled,
And kissing the cheeks of these meek ones, he girdled
The waist of a well-favored daughter with laughter,
Lifting her first, others following after.

# IV
## THE VALLEY OF NIMROD

The people of Jared obeyed God's direction,
Preparing for travel by making collection
Of all they might need, as their wisdom reminded.
Led by a prophet, the band was not blinded

Like many retreating from ruined Confusion,
Who hastily fled from the Lord's revolution
To Nineveh, Calneh, Rehoboth or Resen.
Others would colonize lands of possession.

Though hardly accustomed to rigorous travel
They gladly set forth from the limits of Babel,
Excited to be in the Lord's expedition,
Freed from the palsy of dull indecision.

Their wagons were heaped with provisions they salvaged
By sifting the places the hurricane ravaged.
Surviving the storm, they had worked overturning
Dusty debris, where the fires were not burning.

These twenty-four families, afoot for a schooling,
With elephants helping by forcefully pulling
Long wagons with baggage and tents overladen,
Trekked a track north from the city forsaken

By mild flowing Tigris where grow the high grasses,
Through wild-flowered pastures, whose glory surpasses
The shrinings of Shinar, where sin was devotion,
Vice-groves and gardens for carnal emotion.

Abandoning borders of burnt brick and mortar,
Withdrawn from the sprawl of a fallen disorder,
Removed from the ruins of Babel's rebellions,
No longer governed by high-vaunting hellions,

They walked from the highlands with all of their burdens.
They moved in the hope of their prophet's assurance
Away from perdition, where sin once abounded;
Down from the havoc, where pride lay confounded.

With minds optimistic, they followed for better
The man, whose petition had kept them together,
The one, whom the Lord had commissioned to lead them
Godward to Eden, a nation of freedom.

Shone he with humility, peace, and devotion;
A man of benevolent bent, who below won
Great blessings from heaven above by observing
All the commandments with purpose unswerving.

They transferred a vessel of fresh-water fishes,
And fowls of the air, which they snared within meshes.
All manner of seeds were secured from the farmlands,
Chosen for orchards and vineyards and gardens.

And honeybees, captured in meadows of nectar,
They carried, as ordered by Jared's director.
Beloved deseret, so desired for their service;
Swarming, sweet, wax-weaving bees with a purpose.

They walked to the valley once named for the Hunter,
Whose blasphemous bastion was blasted asunder
By storm winds of towering wrath, armed for wasting,
Quickened to quell Babel's evil upraising.

Now, Nimrod descended the third generation
From Noah. By bow, he made war with creation
And ripened a vain reputation for bloodshed,
Slaughtering animals after the floodshed.

What irony! Leading that seed to the Hunter's
Arena, where Nimrod took pleasure in plunders
And thrilled in the killings of peaceable creatures
Placed on the earth by divine overseers.

The hunt is permitted to satisfy hunger,
But only necessity pardoned it under
The law of compassion once given to Noah.
All have the infinite love of Jehovah.

In fallen dominions, all stewards are tested.
Are Godlike compassion and love manifested
By men in relation to weaker creation?
How are we treating these souls of salvation?

Yes, even the animals God has created
For glory and joy in His kingdom are hated
By Satan, whose venomous jealousy wages
War upon nature through all of the ages.

Belligerent Serpent! His anger and envy
Are sent against heirs of salvation intently,
Those worthier spirits embodied through mothers,
Each of creation our Savior recovers.

The devil of devils delights in destruction.
What misery follows his deadly seduction!
He uses delusion and lust and depravement.
Promising freedom, he leads to enslavement.

And Nimrod was lured into empty advancements,
Rejecting the prophets, who taught the commandments.
When tempted by Satan to lust after power,
Impious plans did he draw for a tower,

A tower surmounting the height of the water
That Nimrod imagined would come to their quarter.
Unlit were the spirits supporting his order,
Dark as the coal-tar they used for their mortar.

His love for authority, riches, and honor
On earth overcame him and caused him to squander
The choices his God-given liberty gave him,
Letting the picks of his freedom enslave him

Like gain-lusting Cain, who took payment from Satan,
The curse of Perdition and honors of Mahan,
Who stained Abel's pasture with sanguine disclosure,
Sure that his murder was hid from exposure.

For Nimrod accused the Almighty of murder
And judged that the Lord in the future would perjure
By swallowing souls in a flood overflowing,
Breaking the oath that He gave unto Noah.

Inimical Nimrod! He cursed the Redeemer!
How sickened was Shem by this wicked blasphemer,
Who swore to avenge the men slain in the Rinsing,
Finding all calls to repent unconvincing.

Combined in rebellion, his vain unbelievers
Refused to resettle beyond the two rivers.
And proudly conspiring, they mocked to their cursing
Prophets repeating God's call for dispersion.

Except for a remnant who kept to the banner,
They answered with arrogance after this manner:
"Has not the advice of our gods been omniscient?
Isn't the word of our wise men sufficient?

Your eyes should apprize you that we have succeeded.
Our houses! Our palaces! All we have needed
Is now by our wisdom and power provided.
Look at the works of our hands and be quiet.

For who is Jehovah that we should obey Him?
What paid He our people that we should repay Him?
We can of ourselves raise a powerful nation
Famous in name and of great reputation."

They flouted the prophets, until the Endower
Came down to examine the city and tower
And found these bitumen-stained citizens failing,
Striving for heaven by means unavailing.

The Lord overheard their abhorred resolution,
Conferred the inglorious name of Confusion,
And aired His contempt for their wicked intention,
Mixing their language from one comprehension.

God swore in His anger that they would be scattered
Abroad on the earth for their violence, which shattered
The peace of the people, who dwelt in the region.
These were at risk from the war-making legion

Of Nimrod, the blood-lusting tyrant of Babel,
Who plotted with others to conquer by battle
And were in their scheming by Satan impassioned.
God brought an end to the things they imagined.

As sinners with singular utterance ranted,
When touched by the Spirit their speech was supplanted
With variant tongues to dissever those errant,
Making the power of heaven apparent.

Then, cold winds collected to blow where God listed,
A phalanx in close ranks, all armored and fisted,
Unleashed by the Lord when His anger was kindled,
Scattering those who in unbelief dwindled.

The baffled ones fled from the terror of Babel,
As chaff from a threshing-floor, fanned like fine gravel,
Beyond the command of that tyrannous Archer,
Speaking mixed tongues at their speedy departure.

Now, down to the lowlands came Jared's procession,
A river of refugees freed from oppression,
All quickened by hope, by obedience banded,
Wending in oneness, as God had commanded.

They halted where treasures of trees in the valley
Afforded a suitable campsite to rally
Their strength after two days of difficult travel.
Many had never yet ventured from Babel.

These suffered the soreness that followed exertion
Beyond their habitual labors in urban
Banality. These before long would be sturdy,
Physically fit for the arduous journey.

The vale was abounding with flowers all over,
A chaos of color on blankets of clover;
A motion of ripples and ruffles unceasing,
Playful and festal in pageants well-pleasing.

And all of the valley lay hushed in a shiver,
Except for the murmuring purl of a river,
That dabbled subdued through the meadow it mastered,
Peacefully laced where serenity pastured.

Who entered surrendered with joy to a vernal
Tranquility, stilling their spirits in fertile
Reflection. And even their children, enchanted,
Greened in the solace the solitude granted.

As quiet as clouds bowed their flocks in the verdure,
Contentedly browsing without a disturber
To hinder the pleasure of rural seclusion,
Pleasure of feasting on scented profusion.

The air bore the essence of flowerful jasmine,
Where gestured the shepherd his people unfasten
Their burdens and wait for the prophesied meeting,
Meanwhile to work and to worship entreating.

They made their encampment from family to family,
And Jared saw all were provided for amply,
That each of the older was happily nestled
After the needs of his tenthold were settled.

The prophet devoted his hands to fulfilling
His duty and care for his wives and his children,
The beautiful flowers of heart he entreasured.
Serving his family with tender unmeasured

Affection that rose from the deeps of his being,
He labored erecting their shelters and seeing
That each in his family had places for sleeping,
Furnishing comfort for those in his keeping.

Then, after assisting his wives and his offspring,
He readied to make an acceptable offering
Of peace and thanksgiving for all of his people,
Stacking the rocks in the manner primeval

He learned by observing his father before him
His father had taught him the sacred decorum
Respecting memorial rites for the Ransom,
After conferring the Priesthood upon him.

The altar he built in the midst of the meadow
Would lift up the sacrifice meant to foreshadow
The love to be blooded to gain our salvation,
Cleansing our souls through His precious donation.

The rocks that he heaped were unclean and uneven
To witness the filth and unfitness for heaven
That marks mortal life in the world's opposition,
Standing for man in his fallen condition.

And when he had finally finished the altar,
As fall's lesser light was beginning to falter,
The prophet assembled the people, informing
All to prepare for the morrow at morning,

The seventh and holiest day, which was hallowed
And blessed by the Lord as the Sabbath, that followed
The well-planned and sanctified work of creation,
Made and confirmed by divine declaration

A day of confession, of prayer, and of fasting,
A day of devotion to God Everlasting,
A day for all mankind to rest from their labors,
Offering their thanks unto God for His favors.

He bade them make ready and bathe in the river
And gather midmorning in reverence whither
The hope of the altar stood steady in patience.
There they would pray on this sacred occasion

And offer themselves with a lamb in observance
Of ancient commandment, set forth for affirmance
Of faith in their Savior. The prophet invited
All to be supple in spirit, united

In love, and the power of pure supplication,
That God would fulfill their sublime expectation.
For God had replied to the prophet's entreaty:
"Go to the valley of Nimrod to meet me."

And then, Moriancumer, sure they had listened,
Gave thanks to the Father in prayer and dismissed them
To settle their hearts for the morn of the morrow.
Some were in doubt but were humble to borrow

A seed of assurance from one they had trusted,
Who always had served them and never had lusted
For power above them, but shared in their sorrows —
Sure as a friend for the haps of tomorrows.

# V
# THE PILLAR

The light of the Sabbath illumined the faces
Of all, when they walked from their various places
To join Moriancumer out by the altar.
There he was ready to help them recall their

Redeemer, the infinite sacrifice needed
To rescue their souls from the holds, which impeded
Their happy return to the presence of glory.
Sorely they needed a Savior! How poorly

They shifted in want of the Lamb's intercession.
Yet, He would deliver them from their oppression –
The power of death over body and spirit.
Those placing faith in the Lamb need not fear it.

A lamb without blemish was chosen for slaughter,
A firstling, a male, for the prophet to offer
With love in the hope of the Lord's visitation,
Humbly with thanks and subdued celebration.

They heeded in keeping this Sabbath day holy.
The sum of their thoughts and behavior was solely
Devoted to worship, to rest, and renewal,
Seeking communion with God through eschewal

Of selfish pursuits and involvements of pleasure,
And making the day a delight and a treasure,
A day to give thanks in the cheer of the Spirit,
Helping each other to keep and revere it.

For they were especially blessed as a people;
The Lord had delivered them out of the evil
In Babel and promised to make them a nation,
Led by His voice to a choice situation.

The service began when the congregants gathered.
The figure was slain, and the altar was spattered
By life from the lamb, with this carmine reminder:
Blood from the body of God would unbind their

Transgressions by mercy upon their repentance.
Salvation would come through the Lord's condescendence
From glory to be the Eternal Atoner,
Dying to don the endowments of Donor

Of purity, power, and glorious purpose,
Of freedom, and light unto life by His service.
For blessings, yes, blessings beyond comprehension,
Come through the love of the Lord's intervention.

Their souls overflowed with thanksgiving to Father.
At heart were they glad to be freed from the pother
Of Babel and brought to this beautiful setting.
Many were moved by the sacrifice, letting

Its sacred, descriptive, and typical meaning
Revive and revolve in their intellects, greening
Their faith in the forechosen Lamb of Salvation,
Stirring the sense of their own consecration,

As if on the altar their beings lay naked,
Exposed to the word of the Lord and made sacred
By willing obedience, spirit and body.
They were an offering, the gift of the godly.

The offering was wholly consumed in the burning,
While they once again in their worship were learning
Devotion, to render their total possession,
All of themselves to their Father in heaven.

Then everyone peered from the sacrifice skyward,
Obeying the loud and provocative cry heard
From one of the keen-sighted children attending.
Lo! An unusual cloudlet descending!

Enwrapped in a nebulous veil unrevealing,
The saints from His radiant majesty shielding,
Jehovah descended to speak to His servant,
Feelings infusing, both loving and fervent.

The One, who is named both the Lamb and the Shepherd,
Kept hid, as He stood in the cloudlet that sceptered
The azure above them that day of expectance.
Surely, He honored their faith with acceptance.

Astonishment stymied the bystanding migrants,
Agape, while above paused that hovering guidance.
And wonderstunned children all clung to their parents,
Fixing themselves to their arms, legs, and garments.

How odd that a cloud would descend so and sparkle!
How strange was the sight of that intimate marvel!
That Godsend, by grateful saints never forgotten,
Looked like a glossy cocoon of thick cotton.

The worshippers wept in the joy of His presence,
Rejoiced for the blessings of mercy from heaven's
Considerate majesty. They had found favor!
Worriment faded away like a vapor

Of steam from a pot on a fire. For the people
Were under the wings of the Lord, and His regal
Attendance restored them in faith and in calmness.
Here was the Lord in accord with His promise,

Confirming the things Moriancumer told them.
The marvelous cloud in the valley consoled them
And led them to kneel and to praise the Almighty,
Causing the pillar to glisten more brightly.

Beneath the Lord's glorious pillar agleaming,
The Valley of Nimrod, with animals teeming,
Became a surpassion of joy and rejoicing.
Reverent hymns were selected for voicing -

Angelical melodies loved by the saintly
And graced with the language of Eden, that plainly
Communicates truth in poetic perfection,
Hymns giving Elohim praise and affection.

When echoed one harmony sounding celestial,
A silvery psalm to an audience bestial,
Then even the voice of the Lord joined the choir,
Charging their hearts with a power like fire.

And all in the dale felt the song of Salvation,
Enthralling their souls with a thrilling sensation
And rendering change over them that did hear it,
Lyrics of peace, deeply piercing each spirit.

Then after their praises by song were completed,
The prophet bowed down with the saints and entreated
The name of the Lord for His promised direction.
Soon spoke Jehovah, whose way is perfection.

Direct to the mind of the prophet He uttered
His voice of instruction in words that were shuttered
Away from the rest of the blessed congregation,
Testing their faith with divine revelation

Confined to the servant, whom He had appointed.
God speaks through His prophet, ordained and anointed
To carry His words in accord with the order
Set by our Lord from the first and the former

Of all dispensations. His message in whispers
Was wonderful: "Speak to your brothers and sisters,
My sons and my daughters, the children of Zion:
Render your love to each other. Enliven

The kindness of love for your God and your neighbor,
And minister good in the name of your Savior,
That you may be mine and enjoy my attendance.
Earnestly center your trust and dependence

Completely in me, in the arms of my mercy.
Then, nothing on earth or from hell can deter thee
From reaping a bountiful harvest of glory.
Know that your God will be going before thee

Through challenging stretches of travel and trial
On lightways of wisdom and seasoning vital
For those who endure to inherit my nation.
Blessings will come after much tribulation.

The way is unsafe and precarious, children.
The route is a passage of death, and that villain
Of villains, the godling of Nimrod, would rout thee.
None of my people can prosper without me.

I warn you of Satan, a son of the mourning,
Whose scheme for dominion and mutinous scorning
Of Father's intention brought heaven to sorrow.
Low hath he fallen! Today and tomorrow,

As always, be sure to ignore him, that serpent,
That master of misery. Shun his recurrent
Temptations. O, let not that dangerous devil
Pull down your souls to his desolate level.

Proclaim to my people that I am their freedom,
And if they will look unto me, I will lead them
That they may become, although demons encompass,
Purified, fit to inherit the promise.

You cannot accomplish by self or persistence
This difficult journey without my assistance.
The best of your efforts with mine are sufficient,
Able to grasp the prosperity distant.

For you must depend upon me for salvation.
My grace shall avail you through mortal migration.
Yes, you must believe and rely on your Savior.
Take, for the sake of your weakness, my favor.

O, come unto me and be humble and willing,
And you shall be counseled, my spirit instilling
Your minds with assurance and wisdom, as needed,
More inasmuch as my counsel is heeded.

And if you are faithful to Father in heaven
And trust in your Savior, then you shall be given
A wonderful land of inheritance, winning
Life in the glorious place of beginning –

A country of trees and of grace unabated,
Where I, in the joy of my heart, have created.
Creation is joy, both the work and perception,
Raising up beauty by light of conception.

Now truly, the souls of my people are precious,
And I will refine you in faith by my threshes
Of sacred adversity during your journey,
Leading you carefully pureward in mercy."

He further declared from the core of His pillar,
"I'll purge all my people as gold or as silver.
Who hopes to be pure will endure tribulation,
Trusting that I can ensure your salvation.

So, humble yourselves as will sheep to their shepherd,
And yield to my counsels with faithful, unmeasured
Commitment, and I, whom you call the Almighty,
Surely will strengthen you daily and nightly.

Now after the Sabbath, prepare for departure,
And gather your creatures together to start your
Adventure of faith from the grace of this valley.
Follow my pillar of cloud and allow me

To carefully lead you through wilderness peril.
My presence and power shall bless your transferal,
As saints of the Zion of Enoch were guided.
Means to accomplish this shall be provided."

His counsel then ended; the pillar ascended,
And, clearly as daylight, the man comprehended
The will of the Lord, which his people awaited.
Standing before them, the prophet related

The kindly, encouraging words of the Savior,
Informing the saints to lay store for the labor
Foreseen for them – after their day of revival.
Everyone minded the prophet's recital.

# VI
# JOURNEY FROM THE VALLEY OF NIMROD

Departing the vale, the disciples were guided
Through places where people had never resided
And places where races had one time been present,
Known by the manbones in chaos quiescent.

A visible cloud God's Begotten enshrouded,
Concealing the Lord from the people of Jared.
The Shepherd's clear voice from His luminous curtain
Made the strait way through the wilderness certain.

They faithfully followed their cloud-clad Redeemer,
As sheep in His shadow, with peaceful demeanor,
Across laky landscapes and desolate spaces,
Water-worn, windswept, and empty-kept places.

He led them through lands where no roadways existed,
Where no one was living. Their column consisted
Of families, wagons, filled up with their chattel,
Elephants, horses, cureloms, and cattle,

And various creatures of every description.
Those animals wilder or smaller were shipped on
Their long-bedded wagons, confined in their cages.
Also, these wagons were most advantageous

To carry their beehives, whenever they traveled
On land. And unnumbered perplexities graveled
Their intellects daily, which stretched them to wisdom.
Questions will always precede acquisition

Of practical knowledge, and these were presented
Through wilderness schooling. By skill, they invented
What tool or procedure their circumstance needed.
Trusting the Pillar, the pilgrims succeeded

In moving the might of their great congregation
Across the demanding expanse of the Asian
Munificence, solving the issues of living,
Working out every distress and misgiving.

All chores were assigned and all labors divided
By Jared, a master of work, who presided
By common consent for communal improvement,
Striving to keep all employed in the movement.

And they were not spared from adversities common
To mankind, yet always a comforting palm from
The tenderest love of another dimension
Softened the pain of their incomprehension,

Consoled them in sorrow, and tempered their trials.
The Lord heard their grieving and gave them the vitals
Of soothing condolence and peaceful assurance,
Helping His people to faithful endurance,

Yes, even through losses of loved ones they buried
In graves by the wayside at times as they journeyed.
To these came the Mercy of Elohim speaking:
"Blessed are those who are called to my keeping."

By pure ministrations of faith, there were healings,
Which also were won by the Shepherd's revealings
Of wondrous medicinal plants and their uses –
Herbage or tubers, the flowers or juices

Prepared in the manner the Healer directed
And likewise dispensed to the person infected.
This curative lore was precisely recorded,
Treasured by saints for the aid it afforded.

And who, save the great and all-knowing Creator,
Could teach them these marvelous secrets of nature,
The potent, remedial virtues He granted
Simply as gifts in the green things He planted?

Through barrens and harshways, they wearily plodded.
Humanely, their lumbering creatures were prodded.
They struggled while trailing the aerial column.
God was preparing these cross-comers solemn.

They trudged through the mudbeds the flooding relinquished
And marched over marshes that well-nigh extinguished
Their will to continue the pilgrimage longer.
Comforting words from the Lord made them stronger.

They suffered fatigue and a wealth of afflictions,
Intended by God to enrich their convictions
And soften their tempers with paramount meekness.
Thus, were the Jaredites strengthened in weakness.

And happily, money was nothing among them.
The sin of division by wealth never wrung them.
Of each was expected his best contribution,
Working in oneness to reach resolution

Of common necessity daily by sharing.
For teamwork was taught with collective upbearing
Of burdens. And naught from the Lord could be hidden.
Greed and its patriarch, pride, were forbidden.

They loved one another and showed it by service,
All learning to conquer their natural urges
For selfish indulgence and proud competition,
Living as children by humble submission

To Him who redeemed them, to Him who descended
From riches of glory in love and extended
The manifold gifts of our Father's affection,
Yielding His will to our Father's direction.

They witnessed the goodness of God on their journey
And found in repentance the blessings of mercy
Bestowed upon those who will honor their Savior,
Call on His name, and improve their behavior.

Thus, eastward the emigrants journeyed, beholding
A distance of wonderful vistas unfolding,
While passing through sparseland, unwooded and spacious,
Pacing through thick-timbered enclaves capacious.

Humility wakened awareness of beauty
And psalmed them to consummate awe from their broody
Communions through year-spans of wearisome seasons –
Beauty abundant that filled their depletions

Of spirit, to lift them in natural wonder
And draw exhalations of gratitude under
The generous hands of their brilliant Creator.
Everywhere, marvels were shown them to savor.

They came with their cattle, cureloms, and cumoms,
A medley of animals useful to humans.
Noachian nomads made plans to replenish
Lands with the living things rains made to vanish.

As Adam and Noah made peace with all creatures
And by pure example became mighty teachers,
The Jaredites, quickened with joy and thanksgiving,
Sought the well-being of everything living.

They teach us that we should with reverence favor
Each creature we eat as a type of the Savior,
An innocent offering meant to preserve us.
Christ is compared to a lamb for this purpose.

These hope-impelled people, of placid opinion,
Attended with tender and gentle dominion
The sweet-tempered animals placed in their keeping,
Serving these creatures and happiness reaping,

Subduing by love every impulse of meanness,
(That enmity Nimrod encouraged with keenness).
They counseled their children to bless the creation,
Acting as stewards for God in probation.

No malice for animals marred the relation
Of saints with those classes of heaven's creation.
And therefore, the Spirit of God, not offended,
Blessed with suffusions the souls He befriended.

Then even the lions were friendly and tranquil,
And neither constraint nor the sword of an angel
Were needed to keep the meek Jaredite shepherds
Safe from the claws of the lions and leopards.

With kindness these treasures of nature were nourished,
And thereby they multiplied amply and flourished.
When herded or carried these creatures, well-cherished,
Went with the exiles, where wildlife had perished,

Reseeding the lands, where the waters receded,
Admeasuring life, as the nomads proceeded,
In numbers and kinds the Creator commanded.
Thus, were the animal spaces expanded.

And various species of fish they thought special
Were caught and collected and bred in a vesse
They carried on one of their wagons the distance.
God had a plan to restore their existence.

And from this aquarium during their travel,
The fish they acquired from the waters near Babel
And elsewhere were freed as the Savior directed,
Stocking the rivers and lakes He selected.

And grasses of wondrous assortment were planted
Wherever the Lord in His wisdom commanded,
With mixes of flowers and herbs they collected.
Thus, was the life of the land resurrected.

At times in their coursing, they came to those quarters
Where they were defied by a baffle of waters
Still whelming the land from the world-wide immersion,
Poured forth to purify earth of perversion.

And rather than parting these seas for the migrants,
The Savior acquainted the saints with the science
Of woodworking, training them how to make barges,
Lakeworthy scows for themselves and their charges.

He taught them production of lumber from timber
And ways of construction both better and simpler
Than they by their reason would ever envision.
Cutting and joining with utmost precision

Were skills that would profit their lives in the future.
They could not appreciate then how their Tutor
Was carefully making them equal to greater
Missions of excellence planned for them later.

Thus, when they were led by the Lord to a lakeshore,
They raised up their lodgings, then set out to make more
Materials meet for the barges they needed.
Seasons would stream by before they succeeded

At building these lakefaring ferries to carry
Their host from the waterfront, where they would tarry
In God-guided industry, tending their gardens,
Caring for creatures and planting the barrens.

They journeyed enjoying delights as they found them
And breathing the breath of the trees all around them,
That rose from the earth in exalted perfection,
Types of the grace of a bright resurrection,

That kept the decrees of creation unsinning,
As God had administered from the beginning.
By His inspiration, they knew they were seeing
Models of Christ in the beauty of being.

Their Shepherd had led them progressively eastward
Across the expanse with their wagons and beast herd.
But if there were murmurs within the procession,
Then they meandered because of transgression,

Or else by their faithlessness tarried or turtled.
Offended, their Pilot no longer encircled
The migrants in safety, and they were afflicted.
Thus, to correct them, their Savior restricted

Their course and their progress, for great is His guidance!
He taught them humility, faith, and compliance
By all that they suffered, in all of their sorrow.
God is a teacher today and tomorrow.

They traveled the verdurous lealands, where plenty
Of herbage and leaflings was life for their many
Companions in ruminant herds, all supported
Richly wherever the Pillar escorted.

Then one day they recognized far in the distance
A mountain range rising with mighty resistance.
They walked on with dazed or uneasy expressions,
Seeing that seeming impassable presence

Ascending like heavenly ramparts excessive,
Supreme in their aspect and deeply impressive.
So grand to their vision that lofty partition!
Awe slowed the steps of the Lord's expedition.

Magnificent vision of glorious giants,
Excelling all grandeur beheld by the migrants!
That beauty, alluring their hearts from their bother,
Filled them with love for their Heavenly Father.

The closer they drew, the more truly colossal
These mountains appeared and increasingly hostile
To progress beyond them. The pilgrims expected
God to direct that their course be corrected

Away from that obvious wall of obstruction.
However, they learned they had erred in deduction.
The Lord, who would school them in faithful reliance,
Ushered them straight to the foot of defiance.

# VII
# MOUNT ZERIN

Forlorn among thorns at the mountains' foundation,
Amazed by the height of those walls of damnation,
The emigrants halted, exhausted and daunted,
Pitching their tents where the pinnacles taunted.

With purpose undone and endurance depleted,
The footsore procession looked worn and defeated.
Each dusty-dim countenance fell in frustration,
Faint from the strain of the lengthy migration.

The mountains, abreast in unbroken succession,
Or shoulder to shoulder in martial compression,
Extended beyond their horizons of vision.
Northward and southward, they ranged without scission.

Arrayed by the clouds, they wore proudly their grandeur,
Displaying the stubborn and confident languor
Of powerful clerics and well-fixed officials,
Grunting the huff of their haughty dismissals

Of those who are lowly and lacking distinction.
A sense of diminishment moved men to shrink in
That arrogant presence that rose like a scorning,
Even delaying the sunlight of morning.

They camped on the skirts of a mount they called Zerin,
Thence sending forth horsemen as scouts to determine
The lines of the land and that area's features,
Searching for food for themselves and their creatures.

And after completing their wide exploration
By horseback along the immense confrontation,
The searchers returned to report observations
Gained from terrain and their arrant frustrations

In finding a passage through thick opposition,
That rose to the clouds with abrupt prohibition
Both northward and southward without termination.
"Why would the Pillar select this location?

Would Father expect us to climb up these mountains?
Yes, surely our Shepherd would make an allowance
For creatures, our wagons, our mothers with children."
These are a sample of thoughts that had filled them

With prickles of doubt, apprehension, and wonder,
While out in pursuit of their circumstance under
Such grandeur that even the language of Eden
Strains to depict that magnificent region.

Then some were unmindful to trust the Almighty,
Who never had treated the people unkindly,
But always provided whatever they needed.
During the journey, their Savior preceded

The pilgrims with wisdom and higher perspective,
Omniscient, and seeking a sacred objective
More vital and fateful than land and a nation.
First among aims of the Prince of Salvation

Is always to strengthen the faith of His people
In Him, their sufficiency, that they might be equal
To all tribulation and all expectation,
Having the power of God in probation.

God's people are carefully taught to rely on
The Only Begotten, like Enoch of Zion,
Whose faith caused the rivers to veer from their courses,
Prompted the wicked to flee with their forces,

Aroused the foundations of earth to convulsion,
And even impelled the dynamic expulsion
Of mountains. For faith is the father of power.
Wonders attend those who trust the Endower.

The cloudy cocoon that conducted the people
Surmounted the uppermost peak like a steeple,
Appearing supreme over towers it crested.
There it remained as the pioneers rested.

For days at the base of the mountains they waited
With leisurely purpose, as weakness abated,
Enjoying a respite, while weariness bound them,
Watching their animals grazing around them.

And soon a new cheeriness shone in their faces,
Their lustrous behavior reflecting the graces
Of deep-seated happiness known to the righteous.
Love over-layered their beings in brightness.

Revived from their travel, the pilgrims serenely
Did witness the kiss of divinity keenly.
In everything visible, infinite beauty
Smiled throughout scenery vital and bloomy.

In due time at daybreak, when they were awaking,
The saints were unsettled by watch keepers making
A clamor in camp, an uncommon commotion.
Quickly men rose to determine what notion,

Annoyance, or conflict, what threat or observance,
Excited those voices and caused the disturbance.
And all who emerged were amazed to the center,
Bathed in the glow of phenomenal splendor.

The pillar that mantled the mountains' Creator,
That glittered in daylight but blazed again later
To signal at nightfall a brighter assurance,
Startled the camp with a morning resurgence

That lit up the morn more than sunlight, transforming
The dimness of dawn for the Jaredites swarming
Outside from their tents to that marvelous vision.
All were surprised by the Pillar's transition.

Seraphic appeared that refulgence exalted,
Begilding the snow-gaudy mountains it vaulted.
The early-roused emigrants worried and wondered,
Squinting to witness the glorywork sunward.

The cloudlet that plumed on the mountains that hour
Had neverfore shone with such radiant power.
They turned to their prophet with anxious expressions.
Humbly to him they appealed with their questions.

"O, why is the pillar so brilliant this morning?
An omen? A witness? Or maybe a warning?
Inquire, Moriancumer! Ask the Almighty,
Why is the cloudlet now shining so brightly?"

He quietly knelt in the midst of his people,
As oft they had seen him since Babel's upheaval.
They joined, while the prophet, with both arms extended,
Offered this prayer, as the Pillar descended:

"O Lord, our Redeemer, please hear our entreaty.
Thou knowest thy people this morn are uneasy,
Because of thy covering cloud which is dazing.
Tell why thy veil like a daystar is blazing.

And if Thou art angry because of transgression,
Forgive this thy people upon our confession.
As long as we turn from the path of our sinning,
Spare us again for another beginning!

Or if thy bright light is not kindled by anger,
But Thou hast bedazzled to warn us of danger,
Deliver thy saints from the evils converging;
Guard us today from an undeserved scourging!"

He ended his prayer when the Lord's easy accent
Distilled in his mind like a spirit relaxant,
Allaying all fear with its mildness familiar,
Calming the prophet below the lit pillar.

The Shepherd thus spoke to the supplicant kneeling:
"Bestill all my sheep from each fear-needled feeling.
Their sins are forgiven; no menace impending
Brightens the face of my presence transcending.

While I, unrevealed, in this coverture hovered,
My weary-worn people with you have recovered,
Regaining the power of will and of sinew,
Girded with vigor, renewed to continue.

Resume then your course to that heritage promised,
For after much effort your purpose is compassed.
Your end is the uttermost part of my vineyard.
If you are faithful, you shall not be hindered."

The smile Moriancumer beamed to the others
Sent peace to the hearts of those sisters and brothers.
Then pausing a moment, the prophet sincerely
Asked of their Shepherd the following query:

"Lord, Thou hast directed the course we have wandered.
Now northward or southward or westerly onward?
We cannot go east through the craggy congestion."
"Eastward, my steward," God answered the question.

"Command in my name that immensity massive.
Command it to move from its setting impassive
Your faith with your priesthood is mightful dominion.
This you shall see when the steep is uprisen."

And then, Moriancumer rose from his kneeling,
As energy flowed to possess every feeling
Within him, a rare and miraculous instance.
Raising his arm, he looked up at the hindrance,

Obstructing the sun and the saints by its greatly
Superlative stature and measure, its weighty
Magnificence east of his East-going people.
God, he was sure, would be more than its equal.

The Prophet, perfervid with confidence certain,
Then spoke, as commanded the Lord from His curtain:
"Mount Zerin, remove, in the name of your Maker!
Zerin depart!" cried the priesthood partaker.

Surprise filled the eyes of the pilgrims assembled.
All fell to the ground, as it rumbled and trembled.
And spellbound they watched from the west of a wonder:
Zerin obeyed and conveyed itself yonder!

Aloft from its footings the barrier lifted;
Away by the power of faith it was shifted,
As if an invisible handgrip stupendous
Easily transferred the mountain tremendous.

And thus, through his trust in the Savior embowered,
The purified Elder, with priesthood empowered,
Like Enoch could overcome nature's debarment,
Wondrously raising that monstrous escarpment,

Creating a passage where none had existed.
Impossible fancy, blind reason resisted!
Impractical wish on a play swing of whimsy,
Hanging delusive by filament flimsy?

No! Faith in the Savior is followed by power,
As fruit of an orchard will follow the flower.
Yes, faith is the father of heavenly graces,
Strength in the truth the believer embraces.

That mountain the power of heaven transported,
Uplifted by man so that man be unthwarted,
In points corresponds to the plan of salvation
Founded for mankind before the creation,

That Christ, as the Mountain of God, would be lifted;
The Guiltless made guilty that man might be gifted
Through Him an eternal advance and advantage,
Thereby the seeming impossible manage –

A passage to mansions of promise provided
Where no way would otherwise be. Man is guided
By God when obedient, faithful, and willing.
God has all power, each purpose fulfilling.

By Christ we are saved. Though our sins be as heavy
As Zerin, our mighty Redeemer is ready
To bear them, to lift them away in His mercy,
Shifting our sorrows that we may be worthy.

By love He provides the approach to progression!
Repent of transgression and His intercession
Atones for impediment sin, which estranges
Children from Father, till they will make changes.

They gladly decamped to extend their adventure,
Commencing a course through the corridor's center
On bedrock unburdened by Zerin's transference,
Leaving a pavement made clear of deterrence.

Transformed by the sight of that mountain exported,
The migrants fared fearlessly forward, escorted
Each step of the trip by their cloud-covered Shepherd,
Brightened by truth and by righteousness sceptered.

Enduring the course of their lengthy migration,
They suffered through every reverse and privation,
Adversity suited to natures unpolished,
Blessing these remnants of Babel Abolished.

The Lord in His might made their cares as a bubble
And carried their souls through those briars of trouble
They oftentimes met in the course of their journey,
Raising a people courageous and sturdy.

The journey was long for the wayworn assortment,
A rigor-fed people of ordered deportment
And vigorous creatures, good-natured and willing,
Slowly by footfalls the distance fulfilling.

A day from the ocean, their cloudy commander
Conducted the band to a mountain of grandeur.
They made their encampment where wonder befell them,
Calling the name of the eminence, Shelem,

A mount of exceeding sublimity, higher
Than any the caravan chanced upon prior.
Yes, surely as far as their eyes could determine,
Even surpassing that runaway, Zerin.

And there in the shadows of Shelem they rested,
While Jared, his brother, and other men crested
That mountain to map out the prospects before them.
Happiness swept through the souls of that quorum,

And all of them wept from their seas of emotion
As eastward they gazed at the glittering ocean,
Surveying a coastland of forest and meadow,
All giving thanks that their band had been led so

Incredibly well by the Lord their Redeemer.
They hastened to tell their companions their dreams were
At hand in a land that was goodly and peaceful,
Simply a day's walk away for their people.

# VIII
## THE SHORES OF THE OCEAN

Approaching the ocean, they heard the surf pounding
And viewed the vast seascape from sylvan surrounding.
Sweet fruit and green beauty bejeweled this region,
Pleasureful pause for the peace-seeking legion.

At last, on the seashore, the Jaredites rested.
The tribe was exhausted, for they had been tested
The long-traveled length of the continent's center,
Rootless since Babel through years of adventure.

They reveled in gladness upon their arrival,
Supposing this country the end of their trial.
They set up their village of joy by the seaside,
Tenting by families, contented and free-eyed

And fervently eager to live without struggle.
Those years in the wilderness, wearied by trouble,
Had made them a people of wholehearted yearning,
Wistful to finish their journey's sojourning

And finally settle for good in that Eden
Reserved for their caravan after completion
Of everything planned for the saints' education,
All that the Savior required of their nation.

To honor their prophet, they gave their location
The name Moriancumer, blazing elation
And thankfulness freely for all of his service.
How they were blessed on those bountiful verges

Confronting the opulent sea! Now their seasons
Of roving were over, they reckoned, and reasons
Persuasive and ample would argue intently:
Stay in this region of beauty and plenty.

The days were alive with unequaled delightment
That seldom could temper the squealing excitement
Of gigglers and gamesters and friskering playsters,
Busy pursuing their sea-lavish pleasures.

The treble-shrill voices of children! Excitement
In young legs and young eyes, enlivened by light sent
To innocence, dancing the joy of their natures.
Listen when happy simplicity capers

Around you with day-larking play and ambition.
For thus was the music and bright disposition
Of youngsters among them – intelligent, vital,
Too full of spirit and health to be idle.

How common a bother of boys in commotion,
Capriciously going from notion to notion
With precious obeisance to present free-being,
Pleasance and play sans parental decreeing!

Soon after the newcomers thronged to that haven
And laid out their dwellings with wagons unladen,
Their Pillar departed, but this was expected,
Once they were led to the land He selected.

Their animals battened on prosperous pasture
Prepared in advance by the provident Master,
Who cares for the creatures within His dominion,
Knows every need in each niche of His kingdom.

Their gardens, not far from their tents, were maternal
To luscious profusion that grew in those fertile
Environs with efforts of simple attention,
Thriving by thickets of wild rhododendron.

Besides what the sea did provide, they depended
On honey abundant from beehives attended
With studied devotion and sweet expectation,
Patient to wait for the luscious donation.

They dwelt in their tents at this wilderness refuge,
Enjoying the beautiful edge of the deluge.
Abiding securely, expecting to linger,
Slighting their Savior, incurring His anger.

Because of their ease, they were slow to consider
The Son, who would drink of the cup, the most bitter,
The One, who would carry these stalled children farther,
Bearing their sufferings to bring them to Father.

By figure, it teaches the Savior would lead them
At last to the greatest most glorious freedom –
The distance in Christ from the pale of salvation
Out to the fulness of bright exaltation.

Their hearts were devoted to swimming and fishing,
To boating the coastline and otherwise blissing
In labors of pleasure and sunny diversions,
Set and determined to limit exertions.

They slipped to a slumber of carnal contentment,
Ignoring the Lord on whom they were dependent.
The spirit of wisdom will make this admission:
Weakness is man in his mortal condition.

In four years of leisure their spirits were sodden,
For they had forgotten the Only Begotten,
The wonders they witnessed, the laws of their Savior,
Wasting themselves by their idle behavior.

Those seasons of ease in complacence and pleasure
Were causing the worst of their natures to fester.
Then Satan had power to foment contention,
Luring the hearts of the saints near dissension.

How quick to forget and how slow to remember
The children of Adam their wondrous Exemplar,
Whose nurture and kindness continue forever!
He is salvation and sole intercessor

For us in the presence of Father in heaven,
Whose sacred profession is making progression
Available, even for man and creation,
Blessing with graces from station to station.

The Lord entertains a superior purpose
Than easy indulgence for souls of His purchase.
He urges the diligent effort essential,
Spurring us on to eternal potential.

And even the prophet had fallen distracted,
As heedless of God as his people. They acted
Like children will, absent their parents' attendance.
Something was needed to prompt their repentance.

The Lord in His pillar returned to the seashore
And summoned the prophet to voice His displeasure
And chasten the man for neglect of devotion,
Slighting the Lord, while he eased by the ocean.

He stood in a glowering cloud oversetting,
Reproving the prophet of God for forgetting
To pray on behalf of himself and his people,
Rousing the saint to repent of this evil.

What shame stormed his soul as he came to contrition,
Rebuked by the Lord for his careless condition,
For each of those derelict days he had wasted.
Knowing his blame, Moriancumer tasted

The bitter infliction of Father's disfavor.
Submissive, he prayed in the name of his Savior,
Imploring forgiveness for every transgression
He had committed — with humble expression

Of sorrow in tears as a child. His repentance
Drew peace from the Savior, whose superintendence
Had borne them successfully forward in mercy,
Leading by love over ranges of worry.

Some notice their peace of a sudden decreasing,
Who have not remembered to pray without ceasing.
For these before long may fall prey to temptation,
Feeling perplexed, in despair and vexation.

And even the prophets of God must be careful
To nurture devotion and ever be prayerful.
The least and the greatest ones — none are exempted.
Prophets, like others, will often be tempted.

He pled for compassion for all at the campsite
For whom he had failed in example, like lamplight
Too dim to be seen, while they eased at the seashore.
Seeking that pardon, he promised to be more

Concerned for his duty to God and to others,
To stand as a light to his sisters and brothers.
And when he had offered his words of appealing,
Thus spoke the Lord to the supplicant kneeling:

"The sins of your brethren and you are forgiven,
Yes, even those sundering sins which have riven
Communion between us, my friend, but remember –
Hearken no more to the voice of the Tempter.

That Serpent is evil, attempting to hinder
My people in progress and kindle the tinder
Of bitter contention within this alliance.
Shelter our oneness by careful compliance

With all my commandments in peace and affliction.
And always be constant in prayer with conviction
That Father is faithful to answer. Believe it!
Ask what is right in my name and receive it.

My Spirit will strive to reprove and awaken,
For verily them whom I love will I chasten.
Now chafe not to harden your heart for correction,
Chasing my Spirit away by rejection.

I showed by the floods the eventual limit
Of patience for those who resisted my Spirit,
When men who were warned would not hearken to Noah.
I am the Lord, and my name is Jehovah,

The Word and the Way of eternal salvation.
This haven is not the supreme destination
Intended by me for this well-rested legion.
I've set thy dwelling place eastward in Eden.

My Son, Moriancumer, brother of Jared,
The land which your people and you will inherit
Is choice over all other lands on this planet,
Blest with the best in abundance and granted

The boon of my promise that those who possess it
Shall prosper forever in freedom invested
By me, by eternal decree and election,
Kept from captivity, given protection

As long as they serve me, the Lord of their nation,
The source of their liberty, power, and station,
The fountain of mercy and life everlasting,
Even their Savior, whose love is surpassing.

However, when those who inhabit my chosen
Dominion have sinned by their wicked devotion
To demons of money and power and pleasure,
Choking with sin to the brim of my measure,

Then they shall be swept from my choice habitation,
Yea, swept as by fire when I send desolation;
Swept clean when I stand as a terrible lion;
Swept by my wrath from the vineyard of Zion.

Keep covenants not to forget and forsake me,
But serve me as servants of truth where I take ye,
And you shall be free from the teeth of oppression,
Succored with blessings in endless succession.

Now, stand an example of living devotion
To say and to do as your Savior has spoken.
Yea, live as a light to my wandering people.
Teach them to love me and overcome evil.

Be good and be happy. For wickedness darkens
The soul like defeat. Yet whenever one hearkens
To Heavenly Father with righteous exertion,
Marrow-deep happiness brightens his person."

For three rousing hours the Pillar proceeded
To speak with the prophet on all that was needed
And all that the Light of Perfection expected,
Giving His charge to the man He corrected:

"Now work, Moriancumer, you and your charges.
Yes, work with your brethren to fabricate barges
Sufficient to carry my sons and my daughters
Over the range of these dangerous waters.

As waters recede from the precincts of Eden,
Which I have reserved for my servants, yea even
A people whose purposes please the Eternal,
Fashion the ships to remove to that fertile

Inheritance far from this passing possession.
Go forth in the spirit of steadfast progression.
I bless those whose efforts are faithfully forward,
Bless those who rise from the torpor of norward.

Be strong in the strength of the Lord, your Creator.
No longer be idle, but joyfully labor
With all of your might to prepare for your transfer.
I will administer means and the manner

Of workmanship strictly from matter to matter.
For all must be done in accord with the pattern
I father with care for the sake of my children.
I am your God and will help you to build them.

Now organize rightly the might of your brothers
To build me eight vessels, each one like the others,
And all in accord with an orderly system.
Carry my words to my friends and enlist them

To consecrate fully their time with their talents
And sacrifice freely an offering of valiance.
Tell each of the souls who would be my disciple,
Rouse from your slumber; no longer be idle!

Awake and arise, all you saints of my kingdom!
Yes, quicken your power and prowess and bring them
With willing intent to the work I command you,
Thereby attaining the blessings I planned to

Bestow upon those who are faithful before me.
Go forth, Moriancumer; work, and then surely
My Spirit and voice will direct you in wisdom.
Say to my servants that I will assist them."

The conference ended. The Presence retreated.
The sandy-kneed prophet, in vigor depleted
But filled with a Spirit that left him light-hearted,
Rose up aroused by the counsel imparted.

# IX
# BUILDING THE ARKS

To counsel the saints, Moriancumer hastened
Ashamed to have been in a state to be chastened,
But grateful for grace that the Holy One granted,
Eager to do as the Lord had commanded.

They gathered around him and sat in their places
With curious looks and concern in their faces,
Aware of the Pillar's return to that setting,
Conscious by conscience of errors and fretting

What message the prophet was given from heaven
Regarding the sins of their leisured regression.
When all had assembled, both older and younger,
Ripe for the words of their sky-faring Wonder,

And quietly ready in mind to be heedful,
He bowed to the ground in the midst of his people
And led them in prayer to the Father offended,
Pouring out thanks for the blessings extended

To them through the years of their wilderness travel,
Since freeing their number from teartimes in Babel,
Providing a Savior to nurture and guide them,
One who gave strength as adversity tried them.

He lengthened their thanks for the wonders and healings
Performed by the power of God, for revealings
Of truth by their Savior, by scripture and Spirit,
Filling their hearts with a hope to inherit

Eternal salvation in mansions of glory,
Made sure by the blood of the Firstborn, by worthy
Atonement preceding His great resurrection,
Bursting the door to the way of perfection.

He raised up their praises, then penitence, praying
Through tears of humility, meekly conveying
The sorrow he felt for forgetting his Maker,
Failing to shepherd His flock, to awake their

Attention to righteousness, prayer, and devotion
To Father in paradise there by the ocean.
And lastly, he asked that the Spirit be present,
Proving the truth of his message by pleasant

Impressions illuming the heart of the hearer.
He closed and then looked upon those who were dearer
To him than the sum of all wealth in creation.
Seeing their tears, he began his relation

Of words from the Holy One, sentence by sentence,
Commencing by urging their humble repentance
Of sins to encourage their rededication
Wholly to Him who had promised a nation,

Exceeding in greatness to them and descendants.
He gave them the word of the Lord of Resplendence
Concerning that purified land with the warning
Voiced as a law for inhabitants scorning

The God of that nation, Salvation Anointed.
He told them the choicest of places appointed
For them and their children lay yet in the distance,
Not on those beautiful shores of sufficience,

But over the breadth of the ocean's immenseness.
They moaned, but the messenger, sensing their tenseness,
Restored them with more of the Savior's instruction,
Telling them God had commanded construction

Of eight special arks, their peculiar erection
According to heaven's design and direction.
The work would take years to perform, he assured them,
Seasons of labor, but God would reward them

Each day of the way for their full consecration,
Each day to the end of their splendid migration.
The Lord their Commander would stand as their Mentor,
There for the sake of their sacred adventure.

"Believe in the Son, and repent of your sinning.
Be done with the pleasures of indolence, stinting
Your growth, like the vines that are choking the oak trees.
Ready your wills for the Pillar, who spoke these

Reproaches with love and with lavish intention
To heighten our lives to a richer dimension
In peace and in place, if we change our behavior.
Otherwise, we will incur the disfavor

Of heaven, yes, even of quickening Adam,
Our Savior, the One who will come on a gladsome
Meridian day as the Lamb of the Highest,
Chosen to suffer for us and to die, lest

The censures of merciless justice should cast us
As cursed from celestial revival. Disastrous
Would this be! Now, let us do better. Then, surely,
We can face forward for grace and for glory."

He finished reciting the words of the Savior
And asked them if they would embark on the labor
Set forth for their good by the Lord of omniscience.
Yes! came the voice of that circle of Christians.

He summoned his brother to come to the center,
Embracing him heartily, showing the tender
Emotion he felt for their bishop, affection
Fervently shared by that noble collection

Of souls Jared cared for through great tribulation.
For Jared was loving, above the temptation
Of power or pride and revered for his service.
Then, Moriancumer stated his purpose,

The will of the Lord for his talented brother:
Let Jared be head of this work, for no other
Among them could organize people as he could,
Order the labor for cutting the tree wood,

And rightly assemble the arks by a stable
Arrangement of teamwork, as Jared was able.
The prophet requested they show affirmation.
Quick came their voices in loud acclamation!

Then early next morning the workingmen gathered,
And Jared assigned them by labors they mastered,
Reminding them not to relax into slackness.
Some men as timber jacks, skilled with their axes,

And others to transfer the trunks from the forest
With elephants tugging the weight of that harvest;
And some to be barkers and wedgemen and trimmers,
Sawyers and lumbermen working the timbers;

Yet others for building a kiln for the lumber.
Then, Jared selected those hands from their number
To locate and level a shipyard on bayside,
Laid out for keeping their work underway wide

Of places where high-flowing water engorges.
He sent forth the blacksmiths to ready their forges
And miners to excavate ore for the metal.
Also, he met with the prophet to settle

What questions he had on that day of beginning,
That day when the colonists turned from their sinning
To labor for Zion in oneness so wondrous.
None were astonished that they had begun thus.

These people were ready and ripe for repentance.
They knew it was time to be brought to remembrance
Of duty and reverence due the Eternal,
Stirring them upwards for ought, a reversal

Of heart from a barren, unyielding direction.
Their prophet's admonishment prompted reflection
And ruffled their beings from numbness and slumming,
Bringing them back to the work of becoming.

Above them, the Pillar of pure inspiration
Remained through those years of the arks' preparation,
Assuring the crews their enormous endeavor
Won them the Holy One's favor and pleasure.

Adept with their adzes, their chisels and mallets,
The diligent shipbuilders filled many pallets
With lumber for ridges and uprights and struttings,
Patterned for frameworks of uniform cuttings.

The labor was guided by Jared, their leader,
Who saw to the cutting of cypress and cedar,
So fragrant and reddish, resisting corruption,
Sturdy and rigid, withstanding destruction.

With rustic devices invented by members,
The shipwrights wrought miracles merely from timbers.
Creating eight transports, with plainness constraining,
Simply depended on Carpenter's training.

And workers of metal, both younger and elder,
Were active with tools at the forge and the smelter,
Well-muscled as models of masculine vigor,
Having the practical strength of a digger.

For digging they did in deposits of copper,
Of iron and tin, also coal, for the proper
Creation of implements, tools, and utensils,
Parts for the vessels and key incidentals.

And now, these industrious saints comprehended
The purpose their foresighted Teacher intended
At wilderness seas, where He gave them instruction
Strictly in watertight woodwork, production

Of seaworthy barges, and patience in living,
Instead of dividing the waters and giving
The migrants a passage on dry ground, or even
Leading them round the great waters to Eden.

Some murmured at times, when it seemed that their Savior
Demanded excessive and difficult labor,
When simpler alternatives gave what they needed.
Now it was clear why the Lord so proceeded!

And now they rejoiced for that earlier schooling,
To know by their practice those principles ruling
The work they were given.  Their knowledge would save them.
Great was the faith their experience gave them!

What words can express our supreme admiration
For Him who redeemed us, the Lord of Creation,
Whose love and intelligence beckon us brightly?
Blessed are those who will trust the Almighty!

Their mallets and mauls made a rumpus of drumming
In uneven rhythms on timber becoming
The ribs and the braces, the brackets and beamwork,
Thumping a pulsing percussion of teamwork.

From sunrise to sunset each day save the blest one,
The sanctified seventh to thankfully rest on,
They tightened their muscles with industry lusty,
Labor that left them exhausted and dusty.

The wisdom of prophets and wise men, recorded
In oft-copied treasures of scripture, afforded
With words of the Lord a sublime education,
Lifting their minds to a rich liberation.

While oft from the clifftops, observers would follow
The frolic of marvelous whales, which would wallow
Below them or surge to the surface, enthralling
All by the wallop of rising and falling.

And common as seagulls were schools of the dolphin
Not far from the shoreline. One watching was often
Beguiled by the regular grace of their motion –
Hilling as if they were stitching the ocean.

Let no one assume from infrequence of mention
The women did less than the men. Their attention
Was constantly spent on the most consequential -
Service essential and vitally central.

They saw to the nurture and care of their children,
For children are vessels more precious to build in
This test time. And many the youngsters among them!
Also, they rendered the diligence common

To women as homemakers since the beginning
Their families' health and felicity hinging
On talents of handiwork, skills of provision,
Having a prowess for cloth and nutrition.

And children would work at the sides of their parents
As scholars of skills in the crafts. Though forbearance
And gentle attention to young ones were needed,
Jaredite mothers and fathers succeeded

In teaching the nurture and virtue of labor.
And thus, were they able to bridle their nature
For folly, while joined in the joy of achieving,
Whether in husbandry, woodwork, or weaving.

The commonwealth busied at bee-bustling tempo,
While affable cattlestock, full of the meadow,
Reposed philosophical after their feeding,
Pausing to ponder the grounds of their being.

The seasons flowed fast for the seaside alliance,
So fleeting was time for these barge-building migrants.
Strong men for the labor, inspired and potent,
Shored by the Spirit's sustaining endowment,

Constructed their vessels with sturdy cohesion
And stalwart enough to convey them to Eden,
Surviving the fury of storms on the currents.
Heaven's design was to see that these servants

Were building their beings as well as their barges.
For faithful obedience always enlarges
The soul of a saint through a progress of graces,
Truth upon truth, as we follow the paces

Established by God with a purpose to lift us.
The Father of Glory is eager to gift us
With all we are willing in Christ to inherit,
All we by grace and obedience merit.

Skilled boatmen worked jointly to build from dried lumber
An octad of arks that could carry their number
Across the wide sea to the choicest of nations,
Promised to them in divine revelations.

The vessels were framed as the Master appointed,
Each perfectly crafted and cleverly jointed,
So seemingly seamless, all edges abutting,
Hulls without fissures by accurate cutting.

With ribs closely bracing, opposing great pressure,
Each lively and lightsome, a tree-length in measure.
No windows, for these would be dashed into pieces.
Peaked at both ends and as leak-proof as dishes.

Each mortise and tenon was pegged and assisted
With cordage created from fibers well-twisted,
Then sewn through the timbers at every connection,
Promising passengers better protection.

Interior cordage and boards were anointed
With vegetable oil, which the ancients exploited
For use in preserving the health of a vessel.
Mopping, they copied a process ancestral.

Hot swabbings of terebinth resin still seething,
An excellent sealant for cedarboard sheathing,
Did deepen the natural red of the siding,
Bodies of shimmering crimson providing –

Each vessel an image of Christ and His mission,
Love's sacrifice seen by the prophets in vision
Preserving believers in coverts of mercy,
Bearing them homeward, through water, when worthy.

Within the eight vessels illumined by candles,
The artisans fastened the last of the panels,
Creating compartments on board for their storage,
Wisely dividing available floorage.

Then scented with cedar and sandalwood shavings,
Enhancing the fragrance of conifer stavings,
The vessels were dressed for the voyage by loaders,
Trimmed with provision to cover malodors.

How happy the day when the prophet inspected
The arks they had finished, as God had directed!
Indeed, they were beautiful, queued by the bayside,
High on their slipworks, awaiting the wayride

To slide down the ramps to the birth of their buoyage.
For soon would the Jaredites leave on their voyage
Across the wide sea to the joy of that Eden,
Promised to them by the voice of the Beacon,

Who hovered above them enveloped in vapor,
Yea, palled in a glorious Pillar, their Savior.
Yet, some were not pleased with the ships thus completed.
These often mentioned the watercraft needed

A medley of modifications for safety,
For comfort, propulsion, and steering, that maybe
The Lord would consider concerns, if persuaded.
How could they travel the seaway unaided

By means to maneuver their arks on the ocean
Or mode for effecting a power of motion?
Like bean pods, their vessels at sea would be drifting,
Subject to float with the whimsical shifting

Of current and wind, so to send them wherever.
They feared the caprice of the sea would dissever
Each vessel from others, unless there were changes
Tending to keep them united on ranges

Of terrible danger while crossing to Eden.
The small alterations they sought were in reason,
They thought, and the Lord would accord with their wisdom,
Letting the builders develop a system

To helm and impel all their ships on the ocean.
Yet, other anxieties troubled the boatmen.
For how would they breathe on this last expedition?
Where were the windows or vents for admission

Of air? When the portals were sealed on departure,
Ere long they would suffocate, far from their harbor.
As fashioned, the vessels were tighter than dishes.
Should they set forth on the dreadful abysses

With no ventilation afforded for breathing?
And what of the odor and ordure? Relieving
These physical needs was a matter essential.
Breathing especially – quite fundamental!

And one more bewildering problem igniting
Unrest in the builders - the question of lighting.
The vessels were swollen with consummate darkness.
How could they cope on the ocean in sparkless

Perdition? Their prophet should take their petitions
To Father and plead that He make those additions
They needed and fix where the ships were deficient.
Yes, he agreed; he would seek the Omniscient.

# X
## ORAH

The next day at sunrise, the prophet departed
From cedar works barefoot, robust, and full-hearted,
On white sand and seaweed, through salt air bemisting,
South by the shoreline on issues persisting.

And eastward, the firmament over the ocean
Wore igneous colors, as if to betoken
A glorious day by such fervent complexion,
Joy in the presence of lofty perfection.

The beach was an image of reasoning arid,
Where needful and kneeling, the brother of Jared,
Who knew by its practice the vantage of praying,
Sought the Almighty in lowliness, saying:

"O Lord, we have finished the work Thou hast given,
Complying with every command, and have striven
To follow precisely thy Spirit's persuasion,
Knowing on Thee we depend for salvation.

Receive now my thanks for the wealth of thine allness,
Bestowed by thy grace in our weakness and smallness.
I humbly acknowledge thy generous favors,
Gifted to us in the course of our labors.

Thy courtesy, mercy, and kindness have kept us
In health and well-being, and Thou didst accept us
Again, when we turned from our careless transgressions,
Changing our hearts, when we offered confessions.

I thank Thee, dear Father, for right of communion
With Thee on behalf of our provident union.
And now, may it please Thee to hear my petition.
Hear Thou from heaven, and see my submission.

The vessels completed are nestled in shoring,
Surrounded by platforms with scaffolds securing.
From forward to aft, they are perfectly fitted,
Seaworthy ships but for features omitted.

The arks are unmasted and oarless, my Master,
And able to fare on the ocean no faster
Than slow-floating driftwood on waterflows wafted.
How shall we travel in vessels thus crafted?

And if we are blest with a method of motion,
By what shall we pilot our ships through the ocean?
Each vessel is helmless, as Thou hast directed.
How shall we steer them with steerage neglected?

Moreover, O Lord, without air we shall smother.
Our barges are closed, wanting windows or other
Contrivance for venting fresh air through the sheathing.
Surely, we need ventilation for breathing!

And lastly, O Master, our vessels are lightless,
So blackish inside them that we would be sightless
The length of the cruise to the land Thou hast chosen,
Groping in darkness while crossing the ocean.

Instruct me, O Lord, how to crown the construction.
Provide this, that we may improve our production.
Upon thine adoring disciples have mercy!
Hearken, O Lord, to thy servant unworthy!"

He ended his prayer, as the Pillared Preserver
Descended. His feelings were surging with fervor.
A Spirit of peace, inexpressible solace,
Cheered him from fear into reassured wholeness.

The prophet's impressible senses were heightened.
His mind by the mind of the Lord was enlightened.
By now, all his worrisome shadows absconded.
Meekly he listened, as Wisdom responded:

"Fear not, Moriancumer; I am your helper,
And I am your progress, your helm, and your shelter.
Seek counsel from me when your burdens are pressing.
Happy are they who rely on my blessing!

For you have I borne from the stars of your starting,
And yours will I steer from the day of departing,
Until you are moored at your new habitation,
Keeping your course by my sure navigation.

Although on the riotous sea I have power
To spare you the ferment of freewind and shower,
'Tis wisdom that you should be finished by friction,
Needful that you be refined in affliction.

That ravening hell of malevolent power
Shall open its driveling mouth to devour
Your fleet in its plight on the face of the plenum,
Arching to menace with enmity's venom.

Believe your Redeemer delivers His servants,
Engendering mercy and granting emergence
From joyless restraint in domains of the Monster.
I shall descend even hellward to conquer!

Although in the breathless abyss you are buried,
And sorrows beleaguer, you need not be worried.
My hands shall extend to the nethermost margins,
Stretching to reach you where misery darkens.

My eyes are upon you throughout your endeavor;
My ears are attentive to hear you, whenever
You pray in my name to our Father Perfected.
Storms may beset you, yet you are protected.

Hard winds on the seaway shall drive you with ardor,
Impelling your vessels from harbor to harbor,
While I, as your steersman alone, will be present,
Guiding my saints to their heritage pleasant.

Your barges, in turbulent waters engirdled,
Or buried, when mountainous surges are hurtled,
Shall be by your Savior assured of survival,
Guarded with care for the promised arrival.

As nautical Noah went forth on the ocean
Without any means for maneuver and motion,
So you shall proceed on the sea unimpeded.
Neither a rudder nor oars will be needed.

I carried the father of this dispensation
Across the Great Flood by my true navigation
Through pestilent tempest to Ararat, even,
Safely to newness and freedom from Eden.

A hole through the bilges of each of the barges
Will give you a way to be rid of discharges
Of waste and will serve as a scuttle for fishing.
Fashion the form, as I show you in vision.

And holes through the hulls overhead will give entrance
To breath for the souls of my waterborn tenants.
When sea squalls befall you with waves overgrowing,
Stop up the air vents to stay the inflowing.

But never unstop both the top and the bottom
Together! This warning must not be forgotten.
If both of the hatches are opened together,
Water will enter and drown you. Remember!

What will you that I should prepare to illumine
Your vessels? You cannot risk fire's consuming
Endangerment. Go not by the light of a fire!
Neither will windows fulfill your desire.

The torrents will batter with windburst and thunder
And threaten to thrash all your vessels asunder.
The glass of your windows would shatter in pieces,
Smashed as the force of the sea storm increases.

What will you that I should prepare for your vessels,
That you may have light in the course of your travels?
Go; study it out in your mind in seclusion.
Ponder upon it to find a solution.

Then, counsel with me after you have considered
In earnest the question before you and figured
A plan or design without windows or fire.
Think, Moriancumer; think, then inquire."

The brother of Jared returned to his dwelling.
His quest to the Lord left a question impelling
His mind on a venture of deep meditation:
How to have light for their sunless migration?

He summoned his brother, the laborers leading,
Then told how the Lord had replied to his pleading
And given him further instruction as needed –
Guidance from God, and the shipbuilders heeded.

With stylus and tablet of beeswax, he drafted
For their understanding the vents to be crafted
In each of the vessels, as God had directed –
Airways and waste holes with stopples connected.

Then after describing the shape, operation,
And size of the vents and their stops in relation,
The prophet apprised them that their pioneering
Rested on God for their progress and steering.

No change would be made to the vessels for motion;
No rudder and helm for traversing the ocean;
No sails nor oars would be needed aboard them.
Trust in the Lord, for the Lord had assured him

That all would be well, if they fixed themselves faithful
On Him, who had blessed them; that they would be able
To cross the wild deep to the promised location.
God would protect them throughout their migration.

He answered what questions he could for the forum
Of curious shipwrights before him, a quorum
As steady in work as the bees in their keeping.
Urging them forward, he ended the meeting.

They went away wondering straight to their labors,
As Jared assigned them, to cut through the layers
Of cedar wood sheathing and fashion the hatches,
Inlets and outlets with lidding and latches.

They left Moriancumer thankful, yet pensive,
Aware that his people were more apprehensive
The closer they came to their vessels' completion.
Some might not come to the lost land of Eden.

Ignoring the chatter of light-hearted children,
The screeching of monkeys, the hammers of building,
He settled in happy detachment and pondered,
Rapt while around him disquiet was squandered.

And there, he sat tethered to thought, unenlightened,
While black-barked acacias beside him were brightened
By flowers of clustering yellow and whiteness.
Light within darkness, declaring its likeness.

No sunlight nor windows nor candles nor torches.
The Lord has forbidden a fire for our purpose
And says that our glass will not last in the sea storms,
Falling on us with the fury of bee swarms.

Then Orah, the first of his wives and the mother
Of four of their children (and bearing another),
Came lightly aside him concerned for his diet,
Softly respecting his custom of quiet.

His tender attendant, unsparing in sparkle,
Aglow in the luster of linen apparel,
Had finished her dinner inside with the children,
Samplings of garden-grow, simple and filling.

Her golden hair, braided with threads of vermillion,
Fell wondrous well-under her shoulders in brilliant
Abundance. And none of her troublesome trials
Shadowed the sun in her eyes and her smiles.

The prophet was roused from his deep meditation,
When Orah caressed him and placed a carnation
Secure in the muss of his beard for amusement,
Making him laugh at her loving inducement.

She nestled beside him with easy affection,
Not prying the reason for his introspection,
But trying to season his thinking for dinner.
Lately, she noticed his figure was thinner.

He told her the cause of his long contemplation:
The question of light for their great emigration.
No windows, no fire, but something far better,
God's admonition to ponder the matter.

Yet all of his thought about light on the ocean
Returned to him simply this singular notion:
Petition the Lord to repeat His expression,
"Let there be light," thus to settle the question.

"If only there shone seven more like my Orah!
Then I, in my shame, would not need to implore a
Long-suffering Father in heaven for lighting.
Darkness takes flight from my beautiful brightling."

She listened with ardent regard to her husband,
Then kissed him a little to end his discussion
And lovingly lure him inside to his nurture.
Seeing her worry, he stood without murmur.

Emerging again at the verge of the ocean,
The moon by her fullness conferred her bright token
And lavished them both in the silk of her splendor,
Charming the lovers to pleasant surrender

In each other's arms for a moment of sweetness,
A moment to savor the wholesome repleteness
Of life with its nectars of checkered adventure,
Bearing the joys of their temporal tenure.

The mouth of the prophet fell audibly open
At words of his helpmeet impulsively spoken:
"If only we owned all the glowstones of Noah."
Stopping abruptly, he stared at his Orah.

"If only we owned all the glowstones of Noah!"
Her comment illumined his mind like a nova
That suddenly surges her light in the heavens.
Shadows gave way to a gush of impressions

That rushed to his reason to cure his confusion.
He knew what to do and could see the conclusion!
Once more he was blessed by her gentle suggestions,
Blessed by another of Orah's conceptions.

For then, he remembered the record of Noah,
Who lit upon grace in the love of Jehovah,
When horrors of darkness enveloped creation,
Cursed by corruption of that generation.

"Of course!" he kept crying with wide eyes and whistles,
Aroused by the thought of those luminous crystals
The Lord once prepared for the ark of salvation.
Possibles kindled his mind, and elation

Like leaven in bread was alive in his being,
For glowstones might furnish the light for their seeing.
Would Father be pleased with his precedent pleading?
Hopefully! Faith only knows by proceeding.

He bowed to his wife near the sweet-scented myrtles,
Then hugged her and kissed her and danced her in circles,
While singing his love to the lilt of her laughter,
Down to the beach where they fell in the water.

# XI
## SHELEM

The sun had not risen again in dominion,
Dividing the light from the dark and beginning
The day, when the prophet set forth on his venture,
Westward away from the settlement's center.

And strapped to the broad of his back were the bellows,
Prepared by his brother with some of his fellows
For blowing the fires in tool-making forges,
Heating the iron from wilderness sources.

At sunrise, he walked through a spreading depression,
Where knobbles of salt from the ocean's recession
In rabbles arose from a surface of purple,
Glimmering softly in ample dispersal.

His excellent habits of health and exertion
Had happily made him a powerful person,
A man of athletic and animate bearing,
Rarely a weakness or sickness impairing.

By regular practice, the prophet was able
To climb with the grace of a deer and to travel
On sandalshod feet for a long-plodding distance,
Reaching the yonders by sturdy persistence.

With confident steps, he ascended the mountain,
Where oft-times the prophet repaired for communion
With Infinite Mercy and Endless Transcendence,
Tutored in mind by the Spirit's attendance.

He made his way carefully over the talus
Of rocky debris leading up to the places,
Where footing was sure and secure if unhurried.
Once in a while he would slip if he scurried.

Midway to the summit, he came to a meadow,
And picking a spot in a juniper's shadow,
He settled to rest among blossoming mellows,
Doffing his gripsack, his backpack, and bellows.

A cave at the edge of the meadow provided
A cover secure, where the prophet decided
To store his essentials and spread out his bedding,
Home for a time in a peaceable setting.

Solemnity tempered the cragged surroundings,
The rugged obsidian cobs with confoundings
Of granite and flint in magnificent chaos,
Jutting about from a natural fracas.

And flowers displayed all their minikin faces
In sweet multiplicity, even in places
Surprising, like odd ones in rockpock reclusion,
Spice for the eyes and the heart in profusion.

Nearby, an ascent leveled off to a terrace
With easterly prospect out into the clearness
Of late afternoon with a view to the ocean.
There, he discovered a place for devotion,

A place where the voice of a waterfall chanted
Her rapturous praise to the Giver, who granted
The wonderful blessings of earth in abundance
Under the glory of heaven's transcendence.

The fountain, which drew from an unseen abysm
And gushed forth her favors in lavish provision
To gladden the ledges with pleasant cascading,
Fashioned a natural basin to bathe in.

A whirliwhiff mist from the waters uplifted,
Confused by occasional windpuffs, and drifted
Through conifer branches with pendulous mosses,
Passing away while conferring its glosses.

He offered a prayer to his Heavenly Father
That all of his weakness in effort and bother
Be strengthened and counted for good and not evil,
Hallowed in power to liven his people.

And then in his prayer, he acknowledged dependence
On Him, who had led them, for God's condescendence
From ultimate glory to walk with His people,
Waking their wills to embrace the ideal.

He soaked in the pool of the fountainhead, sending
His full-hearted thanks to the Source for befriending
His circle of loved ones, his steadfast companions,
Filling the span of his bath with expansions

Of deeply-felt gratitude, naming his blessings –
His wives and his children, his trials and testings,
His priesthood and calling, his strength and well-being.
Thanks to the Father for knowledge, for freeing

His people from Babel, for help on their mission,
For grace on the way of their great expedition.
And thanks for the breadth of experience given
Under the wonderful watchcare of heaven.

"So much to give thanks for! So many the favors!
How generous heaven! What fortunes and treasures
Of goodness and gladness, of truth and of mercy!
Bless us that we may have joy on our journey!"

His words were attached to a catch and a quaver
And tears, when he rendered his thanks for the Savior,
Whose infinite sacrifice proffers to pardon
Every believer forbearing to harden

His heart, the repentant, accepting correction.
What more from the Savior, a sure resurrection
For all, for the good and the evil, reversing
Eden-bred death and her consequent cursing.

He followed the flight of an ease-faring eagle,
Adrift on the aerial seas with her regal
Disdain for the bonds of mundane circumvention,
Weaving her song in the freedom of heaven.

The prophet, at leisure in nature's cathedral,
Imagined the barges had wings like the eagle
And flew with the clouds to complete their migration,
Fleet-feathered home on the winds of elation.

He wondered if people had settled the region
Before the Lord opened the windows of heaven
And poured out His lesson with wet punctuation,
Sending the drenching to end their probation.

No trace or reminder remained of those races,
Which once may have lived in the wide-ranging places
Surrounding Mount Shelem's immense domination,
Nothing to evidence man's habitation.

The thought that he might be the first one to witness
That sunlit magnificence, smiling with riches
Of grace on the ridges and slopes of the mountain,
Filled him with joy, as he soaked in the fountain.

At length, as the ruler of daytime descended,
The prophet, refreshed in his cleanliness, ended
His bath in those waters of pure contemplation.
Wanting the matter to make his creation,

He climbed to a place further up from the terrace,
Where crystals of colorful quartz on the surface
Had captured his eyes on an earlier visit,
Sparkling in sunlight with beauty exquisite.

And once from this garden of gloss, he selected
An amethyst crystal, a gift unexpected
For Orah to wear from her neck as a pendant.
Taking a token of love that was splendent.

He looked through the mix and then broke from a cluster
One six-sided crystal with vitreous luster,
Encrusted with rusty impurities partly,
Judged for the prophet's pursuit to be worthy.

A generous crystal, the weight of a melon,
And one he was certain would liquefy well in
The wrought iron crucible brought for that purpose,
Over the powerful heat of a furnace.

He carried his find to the cave by the meadow,
While clear in his generous mind came the echo
Of words from his darling – "the glowstones of Noah."
Oft in his life would his helpmeet bestow the

Solution he sought, the idea he needed!
The love that he bore for his sweetheart exceeded
His excellent powers of purest expression,
Love to last eons of endless progression.

The next day at breakfast the prophet ate lightly
Then worked to fulfill his intention with sprightly
Enjoyment, as though he expected success in
All of his doing. And nothing could lessen

The animate glow of his confident bearing.
He followed the first of his plan by preparing
The sixteen identical molds for the casting,
Fit for the fluid of glass from the blasting

Of fire on the melting pot. Clay was the matter
He chose for them, knowing a mold will not shatter
If fashioned with walls that are thick and substantial,
Having a hole at the top for a channel

For careful infusion of igneous liquid.
He dug out some clay from the mountain and mixed it
With water in modest amounts, as he kneaded.
Making it supple and sleek, he proceeded

To shape that material wet into molding
Receptacles, balling up handfuls and holing
A hollow in each with a knobby utensil.
Having the cavities smooth was essential.

Then after this part of his plan was completed,
When all of the uniform molds that he needed
Lay ordered in four rows of four where he wanted,
Eager in spirit, the prophet confronted

The next of his project, the need for a furnace.
Experience taught him by feats and reverses
The better design for a wilderness smelter.
This he made ready to serve as a melter

Of natural glass, unrefined in condition,
Like man in transition, awaiting remission
Of sins in that fire of Spirit ensuing
Birth in the waters of sacred renewing.

He shattered the crystalline mass and collected
The pieces to melt in the smelter erected,
Then placed all these bits in the crucible sitting
Fixed on its rocky support as befitting.

With molds in their places and furnace completed
And crystal prepared in the pot to be heated,
The prophet was ready to kindle the burning,
Now for success in his enterprise yearning.

With effort of patience the tinder ignited,
And shortly, the heavier kindling was lighted.
He funneled the breath of the bellows in service,
Swelling the force of the burn in the furnace.

He added some oakwood to feed the combustion,
Attentive to aim each provocative gust in
The rock-girded chamber just under the burning.
This in the past he had mastered while learning

The pure, indispensable art of the smithy,
That crucial pursuit of creation, wherewith he
Had often made implements good and substantial,
Shaped by his work at the forge and the anvil.

His talents were striking in fire beneficial,
Though never before had he melted a crystal,
And nor did he know if his notion was valid.
Noah had glowstones! The concept had sallied

As sunburst will blaze on a cloudy occasion.
It came with unknowing yet dazzling persuasion,
Declining the quiet of hushed inspiration,
Choosing the rush of intense revelation.

He watched as the hue of the crucible altered
And saw that the power of flame never faltered
So close to this critical stage of his labors.
Swiftly, the crystal surrendered its vapors,

Then melted with crackles and cries on the furnace,
And all its impurities rose to the surface,
The rust-colored crust and the drosses that stained it.
Every corruption that clouded or tainted

Its beauty and clarity sprawled like a carpet
Of scum on a lakelet. Now this he discarded,
As man would be rid of his sins by repentance.
Quickly, he scooped from the liquid resplendence

That muddle of crassy debasement and cast it
Away from the furnace that steadily blasted
The base of the crucible. Left was the essence –
Liquefied glass of exquisite candescence.

With caution, he poured the empyreal pureness
At once in the mouths of the molds by the furnace,
Then waited a while for the casting to harden,
Eager to learn that the glass did not darken.

He opened the molds when they cooled for removal
Of all of his beautiful, transparent jewels
He hoped would become, by the Savior's indulgence,
Sixteen miraculous bulbs of refulgence.

Each stone was the size of an egg from a chicken,
And these he would plead with Jehovah to quicken
And cause them to shine by His infinite power,
Trusting his efforts would please the Endower

And prove an acceptable, worthy solution
To answer their need to have light on the ocean.
At sunrise, the seer would make his petition,
Looking to God for a blessing of vision.

# XII
## PRAYER FOR LIGHT

The prophet climbed high for the night, where he slumbered
Just under the summit of Shelem, encumbered
By none of the cares of the previous evening,
Pleased in the peace of his work and believing

The Pillar above him would give His approval
And alter the jewels, providing the crucial
Endowment to save them from traveling sightless.
Early, he made his ascent to the Highest.

He waited to witness what seemed like an omen,
The glorious birthing of light from the ocean,
Then dropped to his knees at the topmost location,
Cupping the stones, as he made supplication.

He cried to the Lord in humility, saying:
"O Lord, thou hast said that thou shalt be conveying
Our ships through the midst of a turbulent ocean.
Shuddersome challenges thou didst foretoken.

And now, be not angry, O Lord, with thy servant,
Because I am feeble before thee and errant.
I know thou art holy and homed in the heavens.
I am unworthy to stand in thy presence.

Because of transgression, man's nature has fallen,
Yet thou hast commanded thy people to call on
The name of the Lord to receive our desires,
Asking in faith as the Spirit inspires.

Because of our sins, thou hast smitten thy people,
Yea, chastened thy chosen, when we were not heedful
To keep thy commandments and faithfully serve thee.
Nevertheless, we have joyed in thy mercy.

Through these many seasons, since leaving the city,
We've lived in the wilderness. Savior, have pity,
And angle thine anger away from thy people.
Soften thy heart for thy servant so pleaful,

And suffer us not to embark on the ocean
In darkness, through tempests of which thou hast spoken.
O Lord, may my faith in thy counsel embolden
Me now. Behold these new stones I did molten.

I know thou art able, and thou hast all power
To benefit mankind from hour to hour.
Then touch, if it please thee, these stones with thy finger.
Touch them, O Dayspring, and be thou the kindler

Of lights for our passage across the abysm.
Give light to our vessels that we may have vision
Throughout our adventure in dismal interment.
Hearken, O Lord, to the prayer of thy servant."

Then after this prayer of the prophet was finished,
When he by persuasions of Spirit relinquished
The sum of himself unto God, His Redeemer,
Suddenly, fear overcame his demeanor

And caused him to fall when he saw what did follow.
The answer he sought came as swift as a swallow,
For Endless extended his hand as was bidden,
Lighting the stones with a finger unhidden.

What light from the glorified stones was engendered!
What stunning effect, when the Holy One tendered
His powerful touch by a finger! It happened,
Bringing to light what he never imagined!

A finger! A finger like that of a person!
A radiant index distinctly emerging
From Godwhere, from mystery's unseen dimension,
Seizing the seeker in egg-eyed attention.

"Arise, Moriancumer, why have you fallen?"
The Savior inquired of the trembling one sprawling
Before Him, whose luminous stones lay disheveled,
Littering light where the prophet was leveled.

Becalmed by the voice, by its mildness familiar,
The same loving voice that he heard from the pillar,
The prophet recovered his confident feeling,
Gathered the stones and returned to his kneeling.

"The sight of the finger of God did affright me.
I fell, when I feared the Almighty would smite me,
For I never knew that my Lord has a body.
Always a pillaring cloud did enshroud thee."

"Because of your faith," the Messiah responded,
"Because of your faith, I have done what you wanted
And shown you my finger, for faith will unhinder.
Did you see more than my singular finger?"

Then answered the supplicant: "Nay; I implore thee,
If I have found favor, then show me thy glory."
"Will you believe all of my words which are spoken?"
Meekly, the Lord God inquired of his chosen.

"Yea, Lord," he replied, "for I know that thou speakest
The truth, as the scriptures attest, and thou keepest
Thy word. I believe thine expressions entire.
Thou art the Father of Truth, not a liar."

And when he had shared his undoubted assertion,
Before him appeared a perceptible person
In stature and form like a typical human.
Verily, more than the stones were illumined!

Jehovah unshuttered the eyes of his querist,
Unveiling the surest of sure and the clearest
Of clear to the mind of the brother of Jared.
Truth! Truth! To what can our poorness compare it?

He saw for himself, was redeemed to the presence
Of God to discover Divinity's essence,
At once all his errors and ignorance ousting,
Losing his faith, for he knew, nothing doubting.

The man was enveloped in glory, transfigured
In light by the Spirit of God, which envigored
His flesh from its natural state to an essence
Sanctified, fit to abide in the presence

Of Infinite Power, whose physical visit,
Uncovered by cloud and in person explicit,
Would otherwise wither and turn him to cinder,
Burned in the blaze of empyreal splendor.

His countenance shone with unusual whiteness,
Beyond the resplendence of sunlight in brightness.
The lackluster cloth of his homespun apparel
Dazzled in glory and brilliance supernal,

Like Enoch the Seer from the country of Cainan,
A preacher and prophet, who found an occasion
On Simeon Mountain to enter that presence,
Clothed in a raiment of light, when the heavens

Unfastened her veils, and he saw the Almighty.
He saw the Almighty and talked as forthrightly
As friend to a friend in a rich conversation,
Facing His face for divine revelation.

"I am Jehovah, the Son and the Father,
The Firstborn of Father above and your brother,
A father to all who receive my salvation,
Life everlasting through my ministration.

Before you were born on the earth, you existed
Throughout the beginning with God, then enlisted
For birth in the flesh with your sisters and brethren,
Eager to joy in the gift of progression."

Then said Volunteer to the brother of Jared:
"The image you see is my body of spirit,
And after my image is mankind engendered.
Bodies of flesh and of blood have been rendered

To be in the likeness and image of spirit.
By faith, you have witnessed that I will inherit
A natural body that looks like my spirit,
Fleshly like yours, when our Father uprears it."

Jehovah unfolded His great revelations
And ministered all through these manifestations
Of truth to the prophet, now bright with discernment.
Strictly, the Savior commanded His servant:

"Now keep these things hidden and safe from the prey of
This sinister world until after the day of
My dying, when I by my own have been lifted
Up on the cross that my own might be gifted

Salvation – forgiveness of sins through repentance,
That they to the mansions of God may have entrance
In glorified bodies restored and perfected.
Treasure my secrets and keep them protected.

Yes, write them in language which I have confounded –
My great revelation – let all be expounded
For later in letters that none can interpret.
Then, when the saintly by righteousness merit

The fulness of truth, I will make my disclosure
Of all you have witnessed with me and expose your
Account by the pen of a prophet, whom I will empower,
Even your story from times of the Tower.

Whoever in faith, not by unbelief blinded,
But meek in their spirits and honestly-minded,
Find treasures of wisdom and knowledge I give them,
Knowledge on knowledge and wisdom on wisdom.

As children of faith, you are gifted attendance
Of precept on precept and doctrine by sentence,
Then doctrine on doctrine to truth in perfection,
Learning the power of prayer and reflection.

Whoever receives this in faith, I will visit
With manifestations of truth by my Spirit.
My sanctified faithful shall see and bear record,
Even as you have, O brother of Jared!

And I have divided my lights from the darkness –
You saints of distinction in shining apartness,
Made pure for the land of Olaha Shinehah,
Leaving the glooms for the glory of Eva.

Your mothers and fathers before the immersion
Were born in that country. They came through the curtain
As spirits from heaven above and were given
Temples of flesh, as your God made provision

Yea, I am your Alpha, and I your Omega
From days when we played in the glory of Vega
To times without time in perfection eternal.
All has been planned for this planet diurnal.

For you are the rays of my joy and my glory,
And surely that season will come, when your story
Shall shine from obscurity, blessing the lightless,
Shine like a sun in the hearts of the righteous."

The Lord gave the prophet the Urim and Thummim,
Two stones called Interpreters, used to illumine
The characters sacred of scriptures long hidden,
Great revelations concealed and forbidden.

These stones were prepared that a seer might manage
To translate the record he'd write in this language
At some future time, when it need not be hidden.
"Keep these stones sealed with the testament written,"

Jehovah commanded the man in His presence.
And then the Messiah, the King, and Quintessence
Of mercy and love from eternal pavilions,
Showed to the prophet that measure of billions

Appointed by Father to dwell on this planet,
The children of God, who were faithful and granted
A temple and time on this earth for probation,
All who would enter through birth since creation.

The interview ended. The man Christ befriended,
Enraptured in body and spirit, descended
From Shelem to take to his sisters and brothers
Sixteen miraculous stones and two others.

Imagine the joy in the breast of that person
For whom the Messiah divided the curtain,
Permitting the prophet to witness His presence,
Peer into sacred things kept in the heavens,

And know, as did Enoch, the truth of our being!
The Holy One could not withhold him from seeing,
So great was his faith and so pure his behavior.
Bright was his love for our glorious Savior.

And thus, from a rock came those graces to lighten
The way, as from Christ come those mercies to whiten
Our souls and illumine the course of salvation,
One Rock to serve for a sturdy foundation.

# XIII
# LADING

The prophet returned to his people from Shelem
With light in his pack and a story to tell them,
Aglow in his face from the glory that lit it,
Speaking of things which the Lord had permitted,

But not of the things which the Lord had forbidden.
For he was admonished that these be left hidden
Till Christ had been killed on the cross, as appointed,
Once that the wicked ones slew the Anointed.

He knew, for he saw, and he often declared it.
A witness that leaked from his eyes when he shared it.
He spoke, as inspired by the gift of the Spirit,
Boldly and clearly to all who would hear it.

The saints were alarmed by his radiant person,
For truly, he looked as if soaked by immersion
In light, in the streams of a glorious fountain.
He was transfigured by God on the mountain!

His countenance shone like the glowstones he carried.
By comforting voice Moriancumer parried
Their terror, though not their inquisitive manner,
Telling his people he met with the Granter

Of light on Mount Shelem, the Lord in the pillar,
Who brilliantly answered his plea to fulfill their
Conspicuous need to extinguish the blackness,
Taxing the vessels they built with exactness

To every specific in plans they were given.
The Lord would not suffer his saints to be driven
Across the infernal abysm in blindness.
Light Everlasting, in mercy and kindness,

The One who created the sun in the heaven,
Had given them glowstones to brighten those ebon
Cocoons that were soon to depart for migration!
All were invited to see the sensation.

A curious circle assembled around him,
And knowing the stones would enchant and astound them,
The luminous man Moriancumer, kneeling,
Opened his backpack, the brilliance revealing,

And spilled out those crystalline eggs of explicit
And plenteous light that were lit by the digit
Of God in His love and His mercy and power.
Faith in their prophet from that very hour

Was settled and certain as sunrise. They marveled
To see the miraculous glowstones unparcelled.
Excited, the heads of the huddle came closer,
Gaping and gawking at gorgeous exposure.

He cheerfully handed the stones to the children
And asked them to pass them around to instill then
In each an esteem for the power of heaven,
Infinite power of Jesus to leaven

Their lives in response to a worthy petition.
He told them aloud that the Lord made provision
For all they would need in the course of their journey.
They would succeed in the arms of His mercy.

And O, the delight in the eyes of the children!
Yes, all of those wonder-dazed people were thrilled and
Surprised that their prophet had taken possession
Somehow of stars from the storehouse of heaven.

He learned that the hatches were nearly completed
With waterproof covers that perfectly seated
And sealed in the manner the Lord had directed,
Keeping the migrants secure and protected.

The prophet instructed that silk-knitted nettings
Be made for the miracles, these for their settings
Suspended from ceilings in each of the barges,
One to an end in the center of arches.

And next Moriancumer met with his brother
Alone in a joyous reunion to cover
The word of the Lord for the work to be finished.
This was in wisdom, for Jared distinguished

Himself as a leader, a worker, and steward.
He wrote down the word Moriancumer tutored,
Recording precisely the counsel as given,
Asking what questions he had in addition.

For Jared had learned to be careful to listen
And knew this was key to a safe expedition.
The Lord is specific and strict in commandment,
Making His promise of joyful advancement

To those who will follow the light of His guidance.
The first of the work for their righteous alliance:
Let hands be appointed to gather the harvest,
Storing it dried in the holds on the barges

In measures He gave for the various creatures
The Savior intended to send with the seekers.
Then see that the best of the livestock is chosen,
Younglings of vigor and fit to be closed in

The vessels the length of their oversea transit.
So many of each, the Creator commanded,
With weanlings of wildlife, from species assorted.
Choice birds and poultry would also be boarded.

"Remember, select from the young of those creatures,
For these take less space and are temperate eaters."
He spoke of the need for replenishing Eden,
Lacking in life from the Flood of depletion

That covered the country, as Noah predicted,
And covered the earth, as their scriptures depicted.
Their vessels were seedpods of life and of purpose.
Eden would flourish, revived by their service!

He gave him a charge to send others to harvest
From garden and orchard and meadow and forest,
Extending their search to the corners of nature,
Various seeds for the land of their Savior.

And foremost, the labor before their departure —
That many be named to prepare and to garner
All manner of food in amounts that were numbered,
Ordered on arks till the larders were cumbered.

When bright Moriancumer fully concluded
Presenting the message, his brother saluted
The prophet with praise and respect, then departed,
Roused by the counsel and warm to get started.

The weeks in the wake of their new luminescence
Were blessed by excitement in work, as the Presence
Above in the pillar affirmed their communion,
Promised by God to the sanctified union.

And Jared's community strictly endeavored
To gather supplies in the quantities measured
For each of their arks, as the Lord had directed.
Colonists hummed to the work and collected

The plenteous yield of their fields for provision
Of adequate food for themselves on the mission
And also, for souls of the animals going.
Jared saw all was prepared for the stowing.

A wave-covered grave did await the brave travelers,
Whose fleet of eight hearses was trimmed for the waters.
With spirits excited, the migrants were making
Plans for the launch of their staunch undertaking.

Each vessel was given a name when perfected,
Names chosen from titles of God, which reflected
The mission Messiah assumed to deliver
Every believer to freedom forever.

Aboard ready barges abiding in dry-dock,
Keen stewards heaved hay sheaves for ravenous livestock.
Fatiguing travail, lifting fall's hefty harvest,
Plenty of provender garnered in earnest!

Cocoons of miraculous silkworms were treated
As delicate treasures in cases unheated,
Thus keeping these chrysalid spinners quiescent,
Objects of care and observance incessant.

And whispery bee leagues, submissively sleeping,
Of bloom-combing, bud-biding enterprise dreaming,
Behaved in their honey rich prisons befitting
Royal-knit cellmates, no trespass committing.

Agreeable sheep, so exceedingly gentle!
Sweet ewes fed their lambs in communion parental
And eyed them with obvious pride and affection,
Taking delight in their black-faced perfection.

And weanlings of much maligned swine were reclining
In girdles of straw-bottomed sties for porcining.
While cuddling in huddles, each dignified farrow
Leaned upon shoat meal to make them less narrow.

And block-bodied oxen stood feasting on fodder,
Concluding the looks of their lodgings were odder
Than anything earthly they hitherto mooneyed.
Foodstuff sufficing, they cheerfully shooflied.

However, the cows, hard-installed in the barges,
Were heard by the crewmates to utter discharges
Of lowing so loud, it behooved much enduring.
Such was the mood of the cows at the mooring.

Their neighbors were horses, by labor well-muscled,
Corralled in unnatural quarters and puzzled.
From forelock to fetlock, they quavered and sweated.
Whining equinely, they whinnied and fretted.

Alas for the donkeys! Harassed and assaulted
By harsh-sounding horses and cows, which they faulted
For having foul humor and very poor breeding.
Stalls kept those cross-tempered herds from stampeding.

Good fellowship followed the floppy-eared mingling
Of jovial goats with their social upbringing,
And frivolous kids, whose behavior elated
Toilers exhausted from moil unabated.

And many the creatures, of every description,
The Jaredites captured and caged to be shipped on
The arks to renew the creation of Eden,
Animals kept for that happy repletion.

In each of the vessels, in rooms interlinking,
Were sizable cisterns of water for drinking,
Enough for the needs of the crews and their creatures,
Filled from the river by hardworking steevers.

All framing and sheathing were finished completely.
At all points connections and panels fit neatly.
Each ship was equipped with provisions sufficient,
Measured by word from their Savior omniscient.

Enthused were the crewmates when lading was finished!
They shouldered the cargo till nighttide extinguished
The lattermost reaches of daylight's ambition.
All of the vessels were filled for the mission.

# XIV
# LAST EVE ASHORE

That last eve ashore found the stevedores cheery,
Although steady labor had left them aweary.
Yet, who could restrain them from singing and grinning?
Ready were they for the morrow's beginning.

And choosing the cliffs for their closing devotion,
A climb overlooking the moonshiny ocean,
They gathered as fathers and mothers and children,
Thrilled by the splendor of heaven's pavilion.

A stellar enchantment befell those assembled.
Entranced, they observed an expanse that resembled
A peaceable sea with the deepness of eons,
Brightly emblazoned by numberless beacons.

The shipbuilders settled with eastward perspective
In stargazing reverie, still and reflective,
As waves on the seashore were pleasantly hushing,
Flowing below them in rhythmic uprushing.

For low was the sound of the push and retreating
Of slow-measured breakers with pulses repeating.
Assembled, the shipbuilders shifted and shivered,
Chilly, yet warmed by the gladness that rivered

Within them like hymns on the eve of their leaving.
They came in humility, primed for receiving
A spur of encouragement facing the passage,
Eager to hear Moriancumer's message.

When all of the clan were together and seated,
The man, Moriancumer, stood up and greeted
His moon-soaked companions in that convocation.
Wishing them peace, he began his oration.

The prophet explained in a language plainspoken
The difficult trials they faced on the ocean,
Then asked them if they would submit to the crossing.
Yes, was the answer of all, none opposing,

For they had been led by the Lord their Redeemer,
Who reared them on miracles worked through their Seer.
From Babel to Zerin, from Zerin to Shelem,
Faith gave the welcome to all that befell them.

He taught them to trust their Redeemer for mercy,
Enduring in faith to the end of their journey,
However unhappy a happenstance met them,
What be the threat or the thrash that beset them.

In cream-colored linen apparel before them,
The prophet continued with humble decorum,
Beholding resolve in both elder and smaller,
Pleased by their manifest courage and valor.

"You children of heaven, endeavor to reckon
The stars in that spangled and sparkling complexion,
The millions of worlds in that kingdom supernal!
Reverence ever our Father Eternal!

For isled in that physical ocean extended
Are orders of planets from which we descended,
Revolving like benison earth in their orbits,
Whirling where Father apportioned their circuits.

Yes, numberless worlds has our Father created,
And some that his daughters and sons be estated
In daylight and darkness, with season and hour,
Coming to pass by the Word of his power.

For, in the beginning the earth was created.
Yes, by the Beginning the earth was instated.
He spoke, and it followed; He spoke, and it heeded.
Forth went the Word, and the worldbirth proceeded.

Behold all those crystalline stars in their beauty!
Behold those empyreal pearls that so mutely
Bear witness of Father's majestic ascendance.
Praise Him, who reigns in the midst of resplendence!

Consider the plan of that vessel of cypress
To Noah revealed by the Son of the Highest,
With uppermost, mid, and inferior stories,
Figured to signify heavenly glories.

In figure of Spirit, the ark is Jehovah,
And it is the covenant God made with Noah,
The Promise with power prepared to protect us,
Lifting our lives with intent to perfect us.

And all but the daughters and sons of perdition
To mansions of glory shall have an admission,
As heirs of salvation the Savior disburses,
Each to receive the reward of his service.

By prophet and scripture to saint and unsaintly
The straitway and wideway are shown to us plainly -
Eternal salvation to them who obey Him,
Endless damnation to them who gainsay Him.

All good is of God, and all evil the devil.
Choose well and receive the celestial level.
Choose evil and forfeit that excellent glory;
Lose exaltation, if we are not worthy.

The meek are not lacking in courage or spirit.
We suffer the world, and if we persevere it,
As harmless as doves and as loving as children,
We will have peace in our Father's pavilion,

The holiest place in the highest of glories,
Where mingle the righteous, who mine from the quarries
Of life and dominion, of joy and rejoicing.
Know that our choices must follow our voicing.

How easy to say we will keep the commandments!
To do as we say, to withstand the entrancements
Of sin and temptation ~ more difficult this is!
Rise in our Savior from deathful abysses,

Not sensual, sinful, shut out from His presence,
But sanctified, fully enjoying His pleasance,
Redeemed from the powers impeding progression,
Flesh as our spirits' eternal possession.

Accepted is he, who believes in the Gospel
Of Jesus, our Savior, who crushes ones hostile
To life through the plan of our Father, defeating
Death and the devil, their evil unseating.

However, belief is alone insufficient
To qualify souls for the life the Omniscient
Reserves for the righteous, the Rest of Perfection.
Those wanting this must comply with direction

Ordained in the councils before the creation,
The law of the Lord to award exaltation –
Repentance of sins in sincerity, fully;
Baptism next by a minister, duly

Empowered with Priesthood, who rightly
Performs the imperative rite the Almighty
Prescribed for remission of sin. Sons and daughters
Must be reborn in the womb of the waters,

Becoming as children, submissive and tender,
Yes, buried, then raised up in newness to render
Compassionate measures of service to others,
Treating all persons as sisters and brothers.

Then, when we arise from the grave of immersion,
Emerging renewed through this gate of conversion,
The guide of the Spirit of God will be gifted,
Blessing our minds with perception uplifted.

Thereafter, the Spirit will spur our conformance
To counsels of goodness and truth in accordance
With all that the prophets have written and spoken,
Growing to godly potential through oaken

Endurance in patience and faith, firm and steady,
From day unto day unto death, always ready,
By willing obedience here, to be taken,
Ready to live with our God, when we waken.

Now, this is the doctrine of joy and the teaching
Of Christ, our Redeemer, to every soul reaching
For life everlasting. How many will listen?
Who will progress on the pathway of wisdom?

We thank the original father and mother,
Who opened the way of progression, that other
Descenders might pass through the gate of begetting,
Freely subscribing for life in this setting.

For Michael is one who is like the Almighty,
The father of many, continuing brightly
In glory forever with vast generations,
Suffering death for the life of his nations.

And Eva, our Mother, who launched our progression,
Still cleaves to her husband, enthroned, in possession
Of knowledge she won in this setting of sorrow.
Let us remember her boldness tomorrow!

We know by His Spirit, the Holy Revealer,
That Father will send forth from heaven a Healer
To salve willing souls with the balm of salvation,
Lifedrops of grace for a perfect purgation.

For He is the Lord and shall yet be exalted
As king on the earth, when the wicked are halted
At last, and the City of God is established,
Joyful in holiness, beautiful, lavished

In glory and love, with the peace of salvation.
The Lord our deliverance, Light of Creation,
Shall yet be exalted on earth as in heaven,
Praised as our King, who has bought our redemption.

For Zion will conquer the host of the villain
And rest on the breast of eternity, children!
Then, we will exult in experience given
Here in adversity leading to heaven.

And now, from the sun of my soul, I assure you
The Lord in His mercy will help us endure to
The wonderful end of the crossing, while living
Calmly, content in the cheer of thanksgiving.

We know Him. Each of us knows Him. We have known Him
Forever. We lifted our hands to enthrone Him,
The Only Begotten of Father. We know Him –
From the beginning, our Own. Let us show Him

Our faith in His power by humble submission
To Him on this voyage of stern opposition,
And bow to His prowess. Let none of us cower.
He is our Savior, our Lord, and Endower.

My worthy ones, virtuous sisters of tender
Emotion, be not worried. Let us surrender
To Him, just as He has surrendered to Father,
Trusting completely. For why should we bother

Our peace and composure by poison of fearing?
Instead, we can choose to be cheerful and cheering,
Expressing our credo by fearless exertion:
God will support us; His power is certain.

We know there are things to be learned that can solely
Be learned in this setting of woe, although wholly
We yearn for our heavenly home, where we started,
Hunger for harmony since we departed.

The stings and the sorrows of being are meant for
Our betterment here in this mortal adventure.
Our bitter misfortunes, in time comprehended,
Sweeten the joys, when our trials are ended.

Our Savior will consecrate all our afflictions
For good, and His care will enrich our convictions
While crossing, whatever the cause or occasion.
This is my witness by Spirit persuasion.

So, we may rejoice in our test of endurance,
For Father has given the sacred assurance
To all who will walk in the way of perfection ~
"Ye shall come forth in the first resurrection."

And we shall be glorified, raised to continue
Forever exalted. Now let this begin to
Refreshen the well of our wills. Saints, be righteous!
Lord, may the light of thy promise excite us!

To God be the honor and glory forever!
May we by the gift of our choices endeavor
To follow the will of our Father and Savior.
Glorify God by our godly behavior!

Our God is our Father, and we are His children.
Yes, God is our Father, and we are His children.
Give thanks to that glorious being above us!
Thanks to the Father who loves us! Who loves us!

To Father be glory and honor forever!
For He shall preserve us and never dissever
Our unions of friendship and marriage unending.
Let us now bless Him with praises ascending!"

They savored the sermon their servant did tell them,
As calm as the honeydew moonlight on Shelem,
Despite the approach of their party's departure,
Knowing their challenges soon would be harder.

Eternity lustered her love like a mother
Caressingly bathing her baby in water,
When each tender person attending that service
Circled to offer a prayer on the terrace.

And tears could be witnessed on all of their faces.
Their spirits were rich in thanksgiving and praises.
The Seer, on his knees at the heart of the circle,
Led them in prayer to their Father Eternal.

"We thank thee, Our Father, for life and for freedom,
For lovingly leading us over the sea from
These bounds of abundance for further refinement.
This is a blessing of heaven's design, sent

To add to our stature, maturing each person
In purity, patience, and faith, which will burgeon
When we will submit to thy care and correction.
Cultivate, Father, our souls to perfection!

And Father, we thank thee for mercy through Jesus,
Without whom the judgment of justice must seize us,
Inflicting the punishment due our transgressions,
Casting us far from thy glorious presence.

Yea, Thou, in Thy love, hast prepared an atonement
For sin by Thy Son to be sent, who alone bent
Beneath our offenses, then slain as the Firstling,
Grants the defense for each penitent curstling.

Now, Thou hast informed me that we shall be woven
As whales among mountainous waves on the ocean,
While furious windstorms and currents propel us.
Help us be faithful, courageous, and zealous.

Our Father in heaven, accept our surrender,
And strengthen our faith through this trying adventure,
For Thou art aware of our worries and weakness.
Be Thou our Guardian over the bleakness

Of ocean, when windstorms are wild and ferocious,
When mountainous waves are upon us. Enclose us
In safety, and bear us at last to our nation.
We are thy children, and Thou, our salvation."

He ended the prayer in the name of the Savior,
And surely, the Spirit assured them the favor
Of heaven would certainly bless their migration,
Sending the calmness of sacred persuasion.

# XV
## THE VOYAGE

A glorious daybreak! A cloudless and flaming
Horizon, where sunrise with passion came shaming
The commonplace blue of the skies inexpressive.
Saints knew the promise, a destiny festive.

They offered farewells, as they went to their places
With many affectionate, tender embraces.
And last-minute gifts were exchanged, as they willed then,
Blankets and sweetcakes and playthings for children.

Then some, who had left the communal endeavor,
Once losing their faith and refusing to labor,
Now, knowing the exodus soon would be starting,
Curious, came to the port of the parting.

The saints were bewildered why these would be hostile
To them, to their God, and the life-giving Gospel.
Now, only persuasion could try to compel them.
Sadly, these stayed in the shadows of Shelem.

O, why do our loved ones deny the Almighty?
O, why do they wander, withholding what rightly
Belongs to our Father - their steadfast devotion?
Why, when He promises Endless promotion?

The ache of this mystery warts explication.
Their excellent faith and obedience blazed in
Our former estate, when those virtues were tested.
How can those same virtues here be arrested?

Whoever desired was permitted a billet,
A berth in a vessel for all who would will it.
And truly, this figures the spirit's decision,
Freely preferred, when the Lord made provision

For man to endure an embodied probation.
Then choosing, the children were sent to creation
In muscle and blood for a temporal tenure,
Bearing the image of God for the venture.

The migrants embarked on their barges, commending
Themselves to the gentle Preserver attending,
Entrusting their souls to the Pillar above them,
Seeing that He condescended to love them.

At last, they set forth for the choice land of promise,
Impelled by their knowledge of God, who is wondrous.
The fetal font-farers undocked for their blessing,
Humbly, like children, submitting to testing.

Then, ministrant winds from the west were beginning
To move the arks outward, concurrently kinning
With current and tide to commence their excursion.
Nervous excitement possessed every person.

A few were unhappy, when they recollected
Those items forgotten or objects neglected,
Those things overlooked in the bustle of leaving,
Left in the village beyond their retrieving.

And these were dismissed from their minds in the offing.
They showed their progressive intention by doffing,
Like Zion, the former for higher refinement,
Following God with contented resignment.

How sorely they suffered soon after departure
From comfort in Port Moriancumer's harbor!
Those frustrating first days at sea! So uneasy!
Bobbing like bubble-glass, quavering, queasy.

While rising and falling like fowl on the waters,
They settled themselves with their sons and their daughters.
God's gifts in their chambers bestowed lithic lighting,
Freeing the seekers to search sacred writing.

All anchored by chronicles authored by Enoch,
Archivist of man's first millennial epoch,
Preserver of histories, sermons, and visions
Treasured for wisdom by earth's early Christians,

And moored by the record of Noah's safe passage,
Whose merciful vessel received the choice vestige
Of air-breathing creatures, by twos and by sevens,
Ark-covered heirs under cloud-darkened heavens,

They taught one another as circumstance granted.
While searching their scriptures, the Spirit implanted
A witness within them beyond contradiction,
Lifting their souls to a buoyant conviction.

Their scriptures included experience given
To them from the time when the tower was riven
To ruin, recounting from wonder to wonder
What they encountered since Babel, while under

Continual care of the gloricus Pillar,
Who saved them from wiles of the wicked ill-willer.
The whole of their seasons, from sunlit to sunless,
Shaped them in holiness, willing in oneness.

The songs sung by mothers helped young ones to picture
Fond epics depicted by prophets in scripture
And fear-calming psalms for the children were choired,
Filling the silence with voices inspired.

God's brooding and breathing primordial spirit,
Which moved on the deep before men lived to fear it,
Once soothed, but now stirred up, the seething sea weather,
Striving in tempest, once tempering zephyr.

As shifting winds wailed to confirm the storm's mourning,
The falling of freight gave the venturers warning
Of gusts, with aspiring ambition, as boastful
As Sumer's oppressor, so haughty and hostile.

Increasing concussions beset the sea shelters,
Uplifted in torment on billows' wild welters.
The waves gnashed upon them, like ravenous masses
Foaming for bread crust cast off on the grasses.

With rollicking wallow and yaw, the flotilla
Would grapple with barreling waves that would spill a
Suffusion, while shudderers suffered the pummels,
Grabbing for handholds in time for the tumbles.

How frequent a pitch of precipitous dipping,
Repeated with alternate lifts, free from tipping!
Untoppled and steady with bows to the heading,
Set by the Lord in the cloud overspreading,

The vessels continued in flawless condition
Across the impetuous sea on their mission
To carry the crews to the haven expected,
Saving their souls with those creatures selected.

The creaking of timber; the clap and the clamor!
The smash and the slam of the thunderstorm's hammer!
The crashing of waves against tightly caulked cauldrons
Drowned out the cries of the cringing young children.

"Be carefuls" were cried when their ballast and balance
Were jounced by the billowing scuds, having talons
That scrolled down in sudden and thrusting succession,
Capping the crabby abyss with aggression.

Encircled by surging assailants in riot,
Scared mariners huddled in hellish disquiet,
As crystalline jewels gave pendulous witness,
Shining on pallid complexions and sickness.

Penned animals trembled and wobbled while bleating,
Expressing their bestial distress and entreating
Their keepers the tempest to stall and make stable,
Hoping to bridle the brutal upheaval.

Incessant the wind! Incessant the whining!
The bellowing inside and outside combining
In ear-jarring argument, rudely unthroated,
Turbulent quarrels the sea storm promoted.

A week and then two and then three weeks together.
The wind seldom ceased in that heaven-stung weather,
That shoved forth the vessels with vehement power,
Much like the vengeance that toppled the tower.

Then thirty days, forty days, fifty days, sixty.
They prayed to obtain their inheritance quickly,
Yet, God thought to prove and improve them in patience.
Father is patient. Ungodliness hastens.

Where patience is waiting, her opposite presses.
Impatience, like Satan, is testy and restless
And willfully must have its way, when it wants it,
Faithless before all afflictions confronted.

But patience is kin to humility, knowing
Our Father is wise and aware in our woeing.
The comfort of scripture affords this assurance:
Father rewards us in faithful endurance.

Then seventy, eighty days, ninety, one hundred.
Though none knew the length of the test they confronted,
The period's period, time to the landing,
Faith was their strength and their rest. Understanding

The presence of God and the plan of salvation,
Encouraged their venturesome souls the duration
Of pent-up dependence, suspended contentment,
Physical stresses, and Satan's resentment.

They welcomed the halcyon lulls for those snatches
Of thankworthy pauses to open the hatches,
Admitting refreshment of airflow and cooling.
Weather obeyed with the Lord overruling.

Whenever the Lord gave relief from the weather,
They never would open both hatches together.
The cap of the scuttle was fastened securely,
Locked and inspected by two to ensure the

Adventurous crew was protected from flooding
At times when the upper was opened. The scudding
Of waves, when the wind would awaken their worry,
Caused them to close up the top in a hurry.

Ah, miserly Death and that soul-hoarder, Hades!
Cruel masters of misery's prisons and cages;
Two spawned at the dawn of our fallen first father,
Adam's descendants each greedy to gather.

Those grasping, grim monsters espied the sea-riders
Approaching like victims for poisonous spiders.
Those life-lusting pirates with pestilent purpose
Fastened dark eyes on the ocean's wild surface.

The belly of hell! An abyss bathed in horror!
The bleak, awful chasm of chaos and sorrow!
Such tempest and tumult, with fierceness and fury,
Sunk the sick seamates in terror and worry.

In bluster and blasting, the enemy boasted:
"Destroy them we will with the strong ones we've hosted!
For none can escape from our ruinous power;
None can deliver whom we would devour!"

These, straining with sinister mission, were spellbound,
With hunger immense, as some mythical hellhound.
Impatient, they waited for waves to make wreckage,
Strewing wet tables with bodies and breakage.

A fathom or further the barges were buried,
Succumbing to smothering seas as they journeyed,
Submersed by the murderous clubbing of breakers,
Laid under waves in the watery acres,

Like caskets entombed in sepulchral commotion,
Interred in that dreadful Abaddon of ocean,
Or cast on the crests by the water's sheer powers,
Shrouded in sheets from high waves and harsh showers.

Like vagabond whales among watery mountains,
They drifted in perils of hell's fatal fountains,
Oft covered in valleys by avalanche crashes,
Down-rushing, seasliding, deep-driving dashes,

Or drawn from the yawning and drowning-deep swellings,
Exhumed by the power of awesome upwellings,
Set free from the whispers of undersea dirges,
Crowning wet summits with breathtaking surges.

Too common these pummels, these rollings, and reelings!
Suspended in nettings of silk from the ceilings,
The glowstones, in tune with the wind's provocation,
Swung out the hours with wild agitation.

The cross-bars above them were thick and substantial.
They hoped that no danger they chanced could dismantle
Their lifesparing transports, so perfectly transomed,
Trusting that they from the depths would be ransomed.

One hundred and twenty; one hundred and thirty.
The vessels advanced on the seaway as pertly
As porpoises, plying the wind-rustled ocean
Potently, just as Jehovah had spoken.

When welter had settled and weather permitted,
When calm overcame the abyss, the well-fitted,
Impervious hatch overhead was unfastened,
Closed when the ocean again was impassioned.

When opened, the top hatch attracted attention
Like nectar to honeybees, prompting suspension
Of chores among some, who would come to the airing,
Breathing the sea breeze received in the faring.

And one at a time would climb up on the ladder
To look on the seascape. Their souls were made gladder.
The joy of fresh air! Cool mist! Full in their faces!
Rapture of sunlight and wide-open spaces!

One hundred and forty; one hundred and fifty.
The circuit of time seemed to trundle more swiftly
And lessen their worry and boredom, whenever
They were engaged in some worthy endeavor.

As part of the chores of each day, they afforded
Particular care to the souls they transported
In cage and enclosure secured in the barges,
Lovingly tending their animal charges.

They captured fresh water in sheepskins suspended
Just under the vents as the godsend descended
Benignly, as long as the sea was not surging,
Catching the rain without threat of submerging.

By lowering nets through the nethermost hatches,
The mariners often were favored with batches
Pulled up from the populous sea by retrievers,
Fish for themselves and their meat-eating creatures.

One hundred and eighty; one hundred and ninety.
Enduring from stonelight to stonelight in finely-
Created conveyance, they wondered and waited,
Nurturing hope in suspense unabated.

Two hundred and ten days; two hundred and twenty.
They tended with confidence, praying intently
In faith for the end of their shifting enshrinement.
Seven phenomenal months in confinement!

Surrounded by muffled and murmurous gurgling,
A bubbling and burbling the crew found disturbing,
They anxiously looked in their vessels for leakage,
Fearing the sounds were a symptom of seepage.

But these were the vessels of heaven's designing,
Exceedingly tight, as are dishes for dining;
Each carpentered close, so no water could enter,
Made to ensure the success of their venture.

The blast of the gales on the boards of their barges
Brought dread to the hearts of the men and their charges.
In tears, they cried out in the name of their Savior.
Comfort and calm were His merciful favor.

Yes, always they prayed as the crossing proceeded,
Beseeching their Father for courage they needed.
Assurance was gifted. The Spirit supported.
God blessed the vessels the Savior escorted.

And gathered like chickens beneath the hen's pinions,
The barges continued through storming dominions,
Propelled past the gateposts of hell and its fellows,
Blown through the roisterly gulf as by bellows.

The deadly abyss did obey the Messiah,
Suppressed with its despot, that hissing pariah,
Eternally coiling in misery dismal,
Foiled by the Lord in the water baptismal.

For no marine monster could mar the Lord's dishes,
Engulfed in the flood in the fashion of fishes,
Nor aqueous weapons could sever wood armor,
Harming the flock in the care of the Martyr.

And monsters there were in those perilous waters,
With tentacles, teeth, and intention for slaughters,
Enormous in size and by nature voracious,
Ripping their victims with passion rapacious.

And thus, were they tossed on the waves of the ocean,
A restless confusion of movement and motion.
By God-given winds on the sea they were driven,
Endlessly threatened, remaining unriven.

Among the travails of the long navigation,
Nativities bore on their hard situation.
But God was a helper for mother and baby,
Held in affectionate arms of His safety.

Their lyrical prayers sweetly cheered fallen faces,
All raising their voices and echoing praises.
The watercraft chorus, soft worship returning,
Sang out together like stars of the morning.

Three hundred days! Losing their verve in traversal,
Some wondered within if they traveled a circle,
If they had been swept to a bleak otherwhereness,
Nervous their Superattendant was careless.

Lo, God is not careless, nor is He uncaring.
No, God is aware of the weight we are bearing.
He works for our progress, with nothing neglected.
He is our Father, forever connected

By spirit that reaches our rivers of reason.
He sees us, our circumstance, history, season,
Our present, and future. His presence is privy.
Hence, is the Holy One able to give the

Attentiveness needed by each of us daily,
Particular care for our fears and our frailty,
According to infinite wisdom and justice,
Knowledge and mercy. Unlimited trust is

Most properly settled in Christ for the better.
To Him for His sacrifice, each is a debtor.
Of course, we are never off-course when we follow
Him, our Redeemer, who loves us through wallow

And woe, in the lowest or crest of our crossing.
In crisis or trial, however exhausting,
Where stamina, patience, and faith are demanded,
He will support us, until we have landed.

Those lustrating, long days at sea! Everlasting
They seemed through the sameness of doldrums or blasting,
Monsoon or monotony, all of it schooling
Saints placing trust in their Lord overruling.

With patience enduring, the Jaredites waited,
Confined in their holds, from the world separated
Like captives condemned without cause for exemption,
Harboring hopes of a royal redemption.

With spirits remorseful and hearts that were broken,
And bending with heads bowed, humility's token,
The pilgrims sought grace from the One with the ransom,
Begging the Savior in safety to land them.

# XVI
# ARRIVAL

The voyage was blest by the Lord their Convoyer,
Whose scepter protected them from the Destroyer
And brought them through hardships to land He had promised,
Mastering surely all threats that encompassed.

The heaven-pressed vessels were washed to their haven,
A shoal near the shoreline, a shallow, safe basin.
Like ponderous clams on the sands were they stranded,
Anchored below by their keels as they landed.

As promised, no power impaired nor impeded.
Their marvelous Ferryman aptly succeeded,
Through pestilent weeks of tempestuous weather,
Keeping the separate sea ships together.

A rigorous trial! A crucial probation!
A Spirit-steered cruise of distressful duration.
Traversing adversity's turbulent water,
Purging the souls of those purchased for Father.

Three hundred and forty-four days for the crossing!
Discomfort and weakness the long voyage causing.
Three hundred and forty-four days for the crossing;
Roughly a year rife with suffering and tossing.

The seaborne disciples rejoiced with deep feeling,
Each humble while leaping, exulting while kneeling.
Triumphant delight for release led to revel,
Loosing excitement subdued by long travel.

What rapturous gratitude leapt from their beings!
Yes, everyone joined in the free-natured spreeings
Of children, indulging in joy and thanksgiving,
Praises and laughter, a freshness of living.

The once-curtained sun by its manner monarchal
Warm-welcomed the newcoming crew with a sparkle,
Delighting with glistening kisses their features,
Sky-smiling freely on arkmates and creatures.

They lit up in spirit and nobody hid it –
"He did it! He did it! He did it! He did it!"
They cried in the joy that their liberty gave them,
Joy in the One, who had power to save them.

Adorned by the colorful arch of a rainbow,
The gladdening gift of medicinal dayglow
Enlivened the happy-eyed rush with its shining,
Joining its light to the joy of their brining,

All knowing the bow in the cloud as a token
To call to remembrance the covenant spoken
By God unto Enoch and Noah concerning
Zion's assembly, her time for returning.

And this is the promise God called everlasting –
The Zion of Enoch with blessings surpassing
Shall one day return from the bosom of heaven,
Joining those people on earth who believe in

The truth of the Firstborn and keep His commandments.
For these, by the Spirit of God, understand whence
They come and delight in the plan of salvation,
Knowing in Christ they can gain exaltation.

The air seemed alive with a spirit redemptive,
A succulent mixture as pure and intensive
As virginal Eden's original breezes,
Heaven-fresh breathing that freedom releases.

Refreshed by the breezes which cooled the white beaches,
Renewed by the sunshine from heavenly reaches,
The Jaredites laughed as they danced with elation,
Joyfully circling for their new creation.

In rapture they capered as happy as aspens
In glorious springlight, when each leaf unfastens
Hosannas to heaven with flashes revoicing.
Even their glistering eyes were rejoicing.

They shed tears of joy for His mercies so tender,
With vows to their Savior of all they could render.
So peaceful the place with no tyrant to trouble!
Liberty's promise increased their tears double.

These people were holy, yes wholly devoted
To Him who forgave them their sins, and were noted
For love set alight by their sanctification,
Souls overflowing with thanks and elation.

Possessed of a happiness few people ever
Experience, weathering well an endeavor
That measured the strength of their faith and endurance,
They were at rest in pure peace and assurance,

As if they had passed at the last into heaven
With light for their robes through the glorious seven
Of Pleiades, homeward to love, absolutely
Soaked in a fulness of infinite beauty.

Thus, those who are faithful in trial are lifted
To dwell in the kingdom where reign all the sifted,
Who follow, like Enoch, God's counsel with courage,
Steering straight courses from mortal to moorage.

You children of faith, who were bathed in the basin,
Were covered by Christ and immersed in salvation,
Laid under the water, then raised from transgression,
Buried then born for the kingdom of heaven -

Our Savior has crucified sin and transgression.
He overcame death, when he made intercession
To save us from these as the Father's Anointed.
Surely in Him is the power appointed.

Consider our souls, as our Father can see us.
Reflect on our hope and our power in Jesus.
For these, whom we name with acclaim reverential,
Help us to reach our eternal potential.

The Only Begotten has lovingly offered
His all on the altar to Father, who authored
The plan of salvation for us who have fallen,
Granting forgiveness to all who will call on

That bountiful mercy by faith and repentance.
Repent having faith in the Son, and that sentence
Of justice offended, which we are deserving,
Falls on the Ransom, our freedom preserving.

Our Savior has called us to life everlasting
As heirs of divinity, all things surpassing.
Though time in this path may be thistled or thorny,
He is our joy and our garment of glory!

Then sing of the Son, His magnificence praising!
With uplifted hearts and with voices upraising,
Sing thanks to our wellspring of joy and of mercy;
Render your love for the One who is worthy.

Yea, sing of the Son and His service availing,
Our generous Savior, whose love is unfailing,
Who came in the image of Elohim meekly,
Earning the power of mercy uniquely.

Lo He, the perfection of excellence, honored
In heaven with Elohim, selflessly sponsored
Our mortal adventure. He Lives! The Atoner –
Chosen and sent by our Father to conquer

Our venomous enemies – Sin, in its varied
And virulent guises, which shackled and carried
So many to prison. Then Death, the unsparing,
All under Adam since Eden ensnaring.

By death we are born into life everlasting.
Now this is the witness of scripture and fasting
And passionate prayer. With the crossing completed,
Truly, the grasp of the grave is defeated.

Through Christ is the endless inheritance given,
For He is the door to the holiest heaven.
He opens the veil to envelop His people,
Saving believers from all that is lethal.

That powerful Seed of the Woman has broken
The poisonous fangs of the Serpent, as spoken
In justice by God on the day of confession,
After the couple revealed their transgression.

For no one can fathom our Father's affection,
Nor sound out the love of His selfless Elect One,
Whose crossing secured us a free resurrection,
Saving His chosen by graceful election.

Though ever so vast the expansive gulf stretches
From earth's teaching seasons to heaven's bleached beaches,
And two-headed Death threatens body and spirit,
We are redeemed through the Mighty One's merit.

## "IT IS FINISHED"

# APPENDIX

## GENESIS 11:1-9

1. *And the whole earth was of one language, and of one speech.*

2. *And it came to pass, as they journeyed from the east, that they found a plain in the land of Shinar; and they dwelt there.*

3. *And they said one to another, Go to, let us make brick, and burn them throughly. And they had brick for stone, and slime had they for morter.*

4. *And they said, Go to, let us build us a city and a tower, whose top may reach unto heaven; and let us make us a name, lest we be scattered abroad upon the face of the whole earth.*

5. *And the Lord came down to see the city and the tower, which the children of men builded.*

6. *And the Lord said, Behold the people is one, and they have all one language; and this they begin to do: and now nothing will be restrained from them, which they have imagined to do.*

7. *Go to, let us go down, and there confound their language, that they may not understand one another's speech.*

8. *So the Lord scattered them abroad from thence upon the face of all the earth: and they left off to build the city.*

9. *Therefore is the name of it called Babel; because the Lord did there confound the language of all the earth: and from thence did the Lord scatter them abroad upon the face of all the earth.* (KJV)

# BOOK OF ETHER (from the Book of Mormon)
## Chapter 1:33-43

*33. Which Jared came forth with his brother and their families, with some others and their families, from the great tower, at the time the Lord confounded the language of the people, and swore in his wrath that they should be scattered upon all the face of the earth; and according to the word of the Lord the people were scattered.*

*34. And the brother of Jared being a large and mighty man, and a man highly favored of the Lord, Jared, his brother, said unto him: Cry unto the Lord, that he will not confound us that we may not understand our words.*

*35. And it came to pass that the brother of Jared did cry unto the Lord, and the Lord had compassion upon Jared; therefore he did not confound the language of Jared; and Jared and his brother were not confounded.*

*36. Then Jared said unto his brother: Cry again unto the Lord, and it may be that he will turn away his anger from them who are our friends, that he confound not their language.*

*37. And it came to pass that the brother of Jared did cry unto the Lord, and the Lord had compassion upon their friends and their families also, that they were not confounded.*

*38. And it came to pass that Jared spake again unto his brother, saying: Go and inquire of the Lord whether he will drive us out of the land, and if he will drive us out of the land, cry unto him whither we shall go. And who knoweth but the Lord will carry us forth into a land which is choice above all the earth? And if it so be, let us be faithful unto the Lord, that we may receive it for our inheritance.*

*39. And it came to pass that the brother of Jared did cry unto the Lord according to that which had been spoken by the mouth of Jared.*

*40. And it came to pass that the Lord did hear the brother of Jared, and had compassion upon him, and said unto him:*

*41. Go to and gather together thy flocks, both male and female, of every kind; and also of the seed of the earth of every kind; and thy families; and also*

Jared thy brother and his family; and also thy friends and their families, and the friends of Jared and their families.

42. And when thou hast done this thou shalt go at the head of them down into the valley which is northward. And there will I meet thee, and I will go before thee into a land which is choice above all the lands of the earth.

43. And there will I bless thee and thy seed, and raise up unto me of thy seed, and of the seed of thy brother, and they who shall go with thee, a great nation. And there shall be none greater than the nation which I will raise up unto me of thy seed, upon all the face of the earth. And thus I will do unto thee because this long time ye have cried unto me.

## Chapter 2

1. And it came to pass that Jared and his brother, and their families, and also the friends of Jared and his brother and their families, went down into the valley which was northward, (and the name of the valley was Nimrod, being called after the mighty hunter) with their flocks which they had gathered together, male and female, of every kind.

2. And they did also lay snares and catch fowls of the air; and they did also prepare a vessel, in which they did carry with them the fish of the waters.

3. And they did also carry with them deseret, which, by interpretation, is a honey bee; and thus they did carry with them swarms of bees, and all manner of that which was upon the face of the land, seeds of every kind.

4. And it came to pass that when they had come down into the valley of Nimrod the Lord came down and talked with the brother of Jared; and he was in a cloud, and the brother of Jared saw him not.

5. And it came to pass that the Lord commanded them that they should go forth into the wilderness, yea, into that quarter where there never had man been. And it came to pass that the Lord did go before them, and did talk with them as he stood in a cloud, and gave directions whither they should travel.

6. And it came to pass that they did travel in the wilderness, and did build barges, in which they did cross many waters, being directed continually by the hand of the Lord.

7. And the Lord would not suffer that they should stop beyond the sea in the wilderness, but he would that they should come forth even unto the land

*of promise, which was choice above all other lands, which the Lord God had preserved for a righteous people.*

*8. And he had sworn in his wrath unto the brother of Jared, that whoso should possess this land of promise, from that time henceforth and forever, should serve him, the true and only God, or they should be swept off when the fulness of his wrath should come upon them.*

*9. And now, we can behold the decrees of God concerning this land, that it is a land of promise; and whatsoever nation shall possess it shall serve God, or they shall be swept off when the fulness of his wrath shall come upon them. And the fulness of his wrath cometh upon them when they are ripened in iniquity.*

*10. For behold, this is a land which is choice above all other lands; wherefore he that doth possess it shall serve God or shall be swept off; for it is the everlasting decree of God. And it is not until the fulness of iniquity among the children of the land, that they are swept off.*

*11. And this cometh unto you, O ye Gentiles, that ye may know the decrees of God—that ye may repent, and not continue in your iniquities until the fulness come, that ye may not bring down the fulness of the wrath of God upon you as the inhabitants of the land have hitherto done.*

*12. Behold, this is a choice land, and whatsoever nation shall possess it shall be free from bondage, and from captivity, and from all other nations under heaven, if they will but serve the God of the land, who is Jesus Christ, who hath been manifested by the things which we have written.*

*13. And now I proceed with my record; for behold, it came to pass that the Lord did bring Jared and his brethren forth even to that great sea which divideth the lands. And as they came to the sea they pitched their tents; and they called the name of the place Moriancumer; and they dwelt in tents, and dwelt in tents upon the seashore for the space of four years.*

*14. And it came to pass at the end of four years that the Lord came again unto the brother of Jared, and stood in a cloud and talked with him. And for the space of three hours did the Lord talk with the brother of Jared, and chastened him because he remembered not to call upon the name of the Lord.*

*15. And the brother of Jared repented of the evil which he had done, and did call upon the name of the Lord for his brethren who were with him. And the Lord said unto him: I will forgive thee and thy brethren of their sins; but thou* shalt not sin any more, for ye shall remember that my Spirit will not always strive with man; wherefore, if ye will sin until ye are fully ripe ye shall be cut off from the presence of the Lord. And these are my thoughts upon the land which I shall give you for your inheritance; for it shall be a land choice above all other lands.

16. And the Lord said: Go to work and build, after the manner of barges which ye have hitherto built. And it came to pass that the brother of Jared did go to work, and also his brethren, and built barges after the manner which they had built, according to the instructions of the Lord. And they were small, and they were light upon the water, even like unto the lightness of a fowl upon the water.

17. And they were built after a manner that they were exceedingly tight, even that they would hold water like unto a dish; and the bottom thereof was tight like unto a dish; and the sides thereof were tight like unto a dish; and the ends thereof were peaked; and the top thereof was tight like unto a dish; and the length thereof was the length of a tree; and the door thereof, when it was shut, was tight like unto a dish.

18. And it came to pass that the brother of Jared cried unto the Lord, saying: O Lord, I have performed the work which thou hast commanded me, and I have made the barges according as thou hast directed me.

19. And behold, O Lord, in them there is no light; whither shall we steer? And also we shall perish, for in them we cannot breathe, save it is the air which is in them; therefore we shall perish.

20. And the Lord said unto the brother of Jared: Behold, thou shalt make a hole in the top, and also in the bottom; and when thou shalt suffer for air thou shalt unstop the hole and receive air. And if it be so that the water come in upon thee, behold, ye shall stop the hole, that ye may not perish in the flood.

21. And it came to pass that the brother of Jared did so, according as the Lord had commanded.

22. And he cried again unto the Lord saying: O Lord, behold I have done even as thou hast commanded me; and I have prepared the vessels for my people, and behold there is no light in them. Behold, O Lord, wilt thou suffer that we shall cross this great water in darkness?

23. And the Lord said unto the brother of Jared: What will ye that I should do that ye may have light in your vessels? For behold, ye cannot have windows, for they will be dashed in pieces; neither shall ye take fire with you, for ye shall not go by the light of fire.

24. For behold, ye shall be as a whale in the midst of the sea; for the mountain waves shall dash upon you. Nevertheless, I will bring you up again out of the depths of the sea; for the winds have gone forth out of my mouth, and also the rains and the floods have I sent forth.

25. And behold, I prepare you against these things; for ye cannot cross this great deep save I prepare you against the waves of the sea, and the winds which have gone forth, and the floods which shall come. Therefore what will ye that I should prepare for you that ye may have light when ye are swallowed up in the depths of the sea?

## Chapter 3

1. And it came to pass that the brother of Jared, (now the number of the vessels which had been prepared was eight) went forth unto the mount, which they called the mount Shelem, because of its exceeding height, and did molten out of a rock sixteen small stones; and they were white and clear, even as transparent glass; and he did carry them in his hands upon the top of the mount, and cried again unto the Lord, saying:

2. O Lord, thou hast said that we must be encompassed about by the floods. Now behold, O Lord, and do not be angry with thy servant because of his weakness before thee; for we know that thou art holy and dwellest in the heavens, and that we are unworthy before thee; because of the fall our natures have become evil continually; nevertheless, O Lord, thou hast given us a commandment that we must call upon thee, that from thee we may receive according to our desires.

3. Behold, O Lord, thou hast smitten us because of our iniquity, and hast driven us forth, and for these many years we have been in the wilderness; nevertheless, thou hast been merciful unto us. O Lord, look upon me in pity, and turn away thine anger from this thy people, and suffer not that they shall go forth across this raging deep in darkness; but behold these things which I have molten out of the rock.

4. And I know, O Lord, that thou hast all power, and can do whatsoever thou wilt for the benefit of man; therefore touch these stones, O Lord, with thy finger, and prepare them that they may shine forth in darkness; and they shall shine forth unto us in the vessels which we have prepared, that we may have light while we shall cross the sea.

5. Behold, O Lord, thou canst do this. We know that thou art able to show forth great power, which looks small unto the understanding of men.

6. And it came to pass that when the brother of Jared had said these words, behold, the Lord stretched forth his hand and touched the stones one by one with his finger. And the veil was taken from off the eyes of the brother of Jared, and he saw the finger of the Lord; and it was as the finger of a man, like unto flesh and blood; and the brother of Jared fell down before the Lord, for he was struck with fear.

7. And the Lord saw that the brother of Jared had fallen to the earth; and the Lord said unto him: Arise, why hast thou fallen?

8. And he saith unto the Lord: I saw the finger of the Lord, and I feared lest he should smite me; for I knew not that the Lord had flesh and blood.

9. And the Lord said unto him: Because of thy faith thou hast seen that I shall take upon me flesh and blood; and never has man come before me with such exceeding faith as thou hast; for were it not so ye could not have seen my finger. Sawest thou more than this?

10. And he answered: Nay; Lord, show thyself unto me.

11. And the Lord said unto him: Believest thou the words which I shall speak?

12. And he answered: Yea, Lord, I know that thou speakest the truth, for thou art a God of truth, and canst not lie.

13. And when he had said these words, behold, the Lord showed himself unto him, and said: Because thou knowest these things ye are redeemed from the fall; therefore ye are brought back into my presence; therefore I show myself unto you.

14. Behold, I am he who was prepared from the foundation of the world to redeem my people. Behold, I am Jesus Christ. I am the Father and the Son. In me shall all mankind have life, and that eternally, even they who shall believe on my name; and they shall become my sons and my daughters.

15. And never have I showed myself unto man whom I have created, for never has man believed in me as thou hast. Seest thou that ye are created after mine own image? Yea, even all men were created in the beginning after mine own image.

16. Behold, this body, which ye now behold, is the body of my spirit; and man have I created after the body of my spirit; and even as I appear unto thee to be in the spirit will I appear unto my people in the flesh.

17. And now, as I, Moroni, said I could not make a full account of these things which are written, therefore it sufficeth me to say that Jesus showed himself unto this man in the spirit, even after the manner and in the likeness of the same body even as he showed himself unto the Nephites.

18. And he ministered unto him even as he ministered unto the Nephites; and all this, that this man might know that he was God, because of the many great works which the Lord had showed unto him.

19. And because of the knowledge of this man he could not be kept from beholding within the veil; and he saw the finger of Jesus, which, when he saw, he fell with fear; for he knew that it was the finger of the Lord; and he had faith no longer, for he knew, nothing doubting.

20. Wherefore, having this perfect knowledge of God, he could not be kept from within the veil; therefore he saw Jesus; and he did minister unto him.

21. And it came to pass that the Lord said unto the brother of Jared: Behold, thou shalt not suffer these things which ye have seen and heard to go forth unto the world, until the time cometh that I shall glorify my name in the flesh; wherefore, ye shall treasure up the things which ye have seen and heard, and show it to no man.

22. And behold, when ye shall come unto me, ye shall write them and shall seal them up, that no one can interpret them; for ye shall write them in a language that they cannot be read.

23. And behold, these two stones will I give unto thee, and ye shall seal them up also with the things which ye shall write.

24. For behold, the language which ye shall write I have confounded; wherefore I will cause in my own due time that these stones shall magnify to the eyes of men these things which ye shall write.

25. And when the Lord had said these words, he showed unto the brother of Jared all the inhabitants of the earth which had been, and also all that would be; and he withheld them not from his sight, even unto the ends of the earth.

26. For he had said unto him in times before, that if he would believe in him that he could show unto him all things—it should be shown unto him; therefore the Lord could not withhold anything from him, for he knew that the Lord could show him all things.

27. And the Lord said unto him: Write these things and seal them up; and I will show them in mine own due time unto the children of men.

28. And it came to pass that the Lord commanded him that he should seal up the two stones which he had received, and show them not, until the Lord should show them unto the children of men.

## Chapter 6:1-18

1. And now I, Moroni, proceed to give the record of Jared and his brother.

2. For it came to pass after the Lord had prepared the stones which the brother of Jared had carried up into the mount, the brother of Jared came down out of the mount, and he did put forth the stones into the vessels which were prepared, one in each end thereof; and behold, they did give light unto the vessels.

3. And thus the Lord caused stones to shine in darkness, to give light unto men, women, and children, that they might not cross the great waters in darkness.

4. And it came to pass that when they had prepared all manner of food, that thereby they might subsist upon the water, and also food for their flocks and herds, and whatsoever beast or animal or fowl that they should carry with them—and it came to pass that when they had done all these things they got aboard of their vessels or barges, and set forth into the sea, commending themselves unto the Lord their God.

5. And it came to pass that the Lord God caused that there should be a furious wind blow upon the face of the waters, towards the promised land; and thus they were tossed upon the waves of the sea before the wind.

6. And it came to pass that they were many times buried in the depths of the sea, because of the mountain waves which broke upon them, and also the great and terrible tempests which were caused by the fierceness of the wind.

7. And it came to pass that when they were buried in the deep there was no water that could hurt them, their vessels being tight like unto a dish, and also they were tight like unto the ark of Noah; therefore when they were encompassed about by many waters they did cry unto the Lord, and he did bring them forth again upon the top of the waters.

8. And it came to pass that the wind did never cease to blow towards the promised land while they were upon the waters; and thus they were driven forth before the wind.

9. And they did sing praises unto the Lord; yea, the brother of Jared did sing praises unto the Lord, and he did thank and praise the Lord all the day long; and when the night came, they did not cease to praise the Lord.

10. And thus they were driven forth; and no monster of the sea could break them, neither whale that could mar them; and they did have light continually, whether it was above the water or under the water.

11. And thus they were driven forth, three hundred and forty and four days upon the water.

12. And they did land upon the shore of the promised land. And when they had set their feet upon the shores of the promised land they bowed themselves down upon the face of the land, and did humble themselves before the Lord, and did shed tears of joy before the Lord, because of the multitude of his tender mercies over them.

13. And it came to pass that they went forth upon the face of the land, and began to till the earth.

14. And Jared had four sons; and they were called Jacom, and Gilgah, and Mahah, and Orihah.

15. And the brother of Jared also begat sons and daughters.

16. And the friends of Jared and his brother were in number about twenty and two souls; and they also begat sons and daughters before they came to the promised land; and therefore they began to be many.

17. And they were taught to walk humbly before the Lord; and they were also taught from on high.

18. And it came to pass that they began to spread upon the face of the land, and to multiply and to till the earth; and they did wax strong in the land.

### Chapter 12:27-31

27. And if men come unto me I will show unto them their weakness. I give unto men weakness that they may be humble; and my grace is sufficient for all men that humble themselves before me; for if they humble themselves before me, and have faith in me, then will I make weak things become strong unto them.

28. Behold, I will show unto the Gentiles their weakness, and I will show unto them that faith, hope and charity bringeth unto me—the fountain of all righteousness.

29. And I, Moroni, having heard these words, was comforted, and said: O Lord, thy righteous will be done, for I know that thou workest unto the children of men according to their faith;

30. For the brother of Jared said unto the mountain Zerin, Remove—and it was removed. And if he had not had faith it would not have moved; wherefore thou workest after men have faith.

31. For thus didst thou manifest thyself unto thy disciples; for after they had faith, and did speak in thy name, thou didst show thyself unto them in great power.

# THE SIBYLLINE ORACLES

*But when the threats of the great God are fulfilled with which he once threatened men when they built the tower in the land of Assyria ... They were all of one language and they wanted to go up to starry heaven. But immediately the immortal one imposed a great compulsion on the winds. Then the winds cast down the great tower from on high, and stirred up strife for mortals among themselves. Therefore, humans gave the city the name Babylon. But when the tower fell, and the tongues of men were diversified by various sounds, the whole earth of humans was filled with fragmenting kingdoms. Then was the tenth generation of articulate men, from the time when the Flood came upon men of old. (3:97-109, The Old Testament Pseudepigrapha. Vol. One, edited by James H. Charlesworth, p. 364)*

# BOOK OF JUBILEES

*And in the thirty-third jubilee, in the first year of this second week, Peleg took a wife whose name was Lomna, daughter of Sina'ar. And she bore a son for him in the fourth year of that week. And he called him Reu because, he said, "Behold, the sons of man have become evil with perverse counsel so that they are building a city and tower for themselves in the land of Shinar. For they departed from the land of Ararat toward the east into Shinar, because in his days they built a city and a tower, saying, "Come let us go up in it into heaven." And they began building. And in the fourth week they baked bricks in fire, and bricks were for them like stones. And the mud with which they plastered was bitumen, which came out of the sea, and the springs of water in the land of Shinar. And they built it; forty-three years they were building it. Its width was two hundred and three bricks. And the height of a brick was one third its length. Five thousand, four hundred and thirty-three cubits and two palms its height rose up. And thirteen stades was its wall. And the Lord our God said to us, "Behold, the people are one and they have begun working. Now nothing will escape them. Behold, let us go down, and let us mix up their tongues so each one will not hear another's word, and they will be scattered into cities and nations, and, therefore, one counsel will not reside with them until the day of judgment." And the Lord went down, and we went down with him. And we saw the city and the tower which the sons of men had built. And he mixed up their tongues, and, therefore, one did not hear another's word. And so they ceased to build the city and the tower. Therefore, all of the land of Shinar is called Babel because there the Lord mixed up all the languages of the sons of men. And from there they were scattered into their cities according to each of their languages and nations. And the Lord sent a great wind upon the tower and overthrew it on the earth. And behold, it is between Asshur and Babylon in the land of Shinar, and he called it "the Overthrow."* (Jubilees 10:18-26, The Old Testament Pseudepigrapha, Volume Two, James H. Charlesworth, pp. 76-77)

# JOSEPHUS, THE ANTIQUITIES OF THE JEWS

*1. Now the sons of Noah were three, - Shem, Japhet, and Ham, born one hundred years before the Deluge. These first of all descended from the mountains into the plains, and fixed their habitation there; and persuaded others who were greatly afraid of the lower grounds on account of the flood, and so were very loath to come down from the higher places, to venture to follow their examples. Now the plain in which they first dwelt was called Shinar. God also commanded them to send colonies abroad, for the thorough peopling of the earth, that they might not raise seditions among themselves, but might cultivate a great part of the earth, and enjoy its fruits after a plentiful manner. But they were so ill instructed that they did not obey God; for which reason they fell into calamities, and were made sensible, by experience, of what sin they had been guilty: for when they flourished with a numerous youth, God admonished them again to send out colonies; but they, imagining the prosperity they enjoyed was not derived from the favor of God, but supposing that their own power was the proper cause of the plentiful condition they were in, did not obey him. Nay, they added to this their disobedience to the Divine will, the suspicion that they were therefore ordered to send out separate colonies, that, being divided asunder, they might the more easily be Oppressed.*

*2. Now it was Nimrod who excited them to such an affront and contempt of God. He was the grandson of Ham, the son of Noah, a bold man, and of great strength of hand. He persuaded them not to ascribe it to God, as if it was through his means they were happy, but to believe that it was their own courage which procured that happiness. He also gradually changed the government into tyranny, seeing no other way of turning men from the fear of God, but to bring them into a constant dependence on his power. He also said he would be revenged on God, if he should have a mind to drown the world again; for that he would build a tower too high for the waters to be able to reach! and that he would avenge himself on God for destroying their forefathers!*

*3. Now the multitude were very ready to follow the determination of Nimrod, and to esteem it a piece of cowardice to submit to God; and they built a tower, neither sparing any pains, nor being in any degree negligent about the work: and, by reason of the multitude of hands employed in it, it grew very high, sooner than anyone could expect; but the thickness of it was so great, and it was so strongly built, that thereby its great height seemed, upon the view, to be less than it really was. It was built of burnt brick, cemented together with mortar, made of bitumen, that it might not be liable to admit water. When God saw that they acted so madly, he did not resolve to destroy them utterly, since they were not grown wiser by the destruction of the former sinners; but he caused a tumult among them, by producing in them divers languages, and causing that, through the multitude of those languages, they should not be able to understand one another. The place wherein they built the tower is now called Babylon, because of the confusion of that language which they readily understood before; for the Hebrews mean by the word Babel, confusion. The Sibyl also makes mention of this tower, and of the confusion of the language, when* she says thus: *"When all men were of one language, some of them built a high tower, as if they would thereby ascend up to heaven, but the gods sent storms of wind and overthrew the tower, and gave every one his peculiar language; and for this reason it was that the city was called Babylon."* But as to the plan of Shinar, in the country of Babylonia, Hestiaeus mentions it, when he says thus: *"Such of the priests as were saved, took the sacred vessels of Jupiter Enyalius, and came to Shinar of Babylonia."*

## Chapter 5

*1. After this they were dispersed abroad, on account of their languages, and went out by colonies everywhere; and each colony took possession of that land which they light upon, and unto which God led them; so that the whole continent was filled with them, both the inland and the maritime countries. There were some also who passed over the sea in ships, and inhabited the islands: and some of those nations do still retain the denominations which were given them by their first founders; but some have lost them also, and some have only admitted certain changes in them, that they might be the more intelligible to the inhabitants. And they were the Greeks who became the authors of such mutations. For when in after-ages they grew potent, they claimed to themselves the glory of antiquity; giving names to the nations that sounded well (in Greek) that they might be better understood among themselves; and setting agreeable forms of government over them, as if they were a people derived from themselves. (The Antiquities of the Jews, in The Works of Josephus, translated by William Whiston, Book 1, Chapters 4 and 5).*

# EUSEBIUS

*They say that the first inhabitants of the earth, glorying in their own strength and size and despising the gods, undertook to raise a tower whose top should reach the sky, in the place in which Babylon now stands; but when it approached the heaven the winds assisted the gods, and overthrew the work upon its contrivers, and its ruins are said to be still at Babylon; and the gods introduced a diversity of tongues among men, who till that time had all spoken the same language; and a war arose between Cronos and Titan. The place in which they built the tower is now called Babylon on account of the confusion of tongues, for confusion is by the Hebrews called Babel. (Eusebius, Præparatio Evangelica, lib. ix)*

# EUPOLEMUS

*The city of Babylon owes its foundation to those who were saved from the catastrophe of the deluge: they were the Giants, and they built the tower which is noticed in history. But the tower being overthrown by the interposition of God, the Giants were scattered over all the earth. (Eusebius, Præparatio Evangelica, lib. ix)*

# APOCALYPSE OF BARUCH

*Those who gave counsel to build the tower, for they whom thou seest drove forth multitudes of both men and women, to make bricks; among whom, a woman making bricks was not allowed to be released in the hour of child-birth, but brought forth while she was making bricks, and carried her child in her apron, and continued to make bricks. And the Lord appeared to them and confused their speech, when they had built the tower to the height of four hundred and sixty-three cubits. And they took a gimlet, and sought to pierce the heavens, saying, Let us see (whether) the heaven is made of clay, or of brass, or of iron. When God saw this He did not permit them, but smote them with blindness and confusion of speech, and rendered them as thou seest. (Greek Apocalypse of Baruch, 3:5-8)*

www.ingramcontent.com/pod-product-compliance
Lightning Source LLC
LaVergne TN
LVHW042244070526
838201LV00088B/20